Christian Liberty Nature Reader

Book Three

Written by
Julia McNair Wright

Revised and Edited by
Edward J. Shewan

Christian Liberty Press
Arlington Heights, Illinois

A publication of
Christian Liberty Press
502 West Euclid Avenue
Arlington Heights, IL 60004
www.christianlibertypress.com

General editorship by Michael J. McHugh
Written by Julia McNair Wright
Revised and edited by Edward J. Shewan
Copyediting by Diane C. Olson
Cover design by Eric D. Bristley
Layout and graphics by Edward J. Shewan

ISBN 978-1-930092-53-2
      1-930092-53-9

Printed in the United States of America

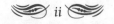

TABLE OF CONTENTS

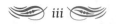

Preface

We are honored to bring you a classic textbook. This particular textbook is designed to not only improve a student's reading skills and comprehension, but to also increase the student's understanding of and interest in God's wonderful creation.

To be able to read is to have the foundation for all subsequent education. The child whose reading training is deficient grows up to become the child who is frustrated, in despair, and soon to join the ranks of the drop-outs, the pushed-outs, the unemployed and the unemployable.

Millions of Americans are handicapped in their reading skills. The "look-say" method of teaching, rather than the older "phonics" technique, has resulted in a generation of functional illiterates. It has been revealed that the U.S. literacy rate has dropped to the level of Burma and Albania and is rapidly approaching that of Zambia.

Not only is the method of teaching reading of vital importance, but also the literary quality of the reading material. So much of what passes for "modern" readers in education today is nothing more than pablum that stresses "social adjustment".

The Bible says we are to do "all for the glory of God" (I Corinthians 10:31). Reading for God's glory necessitates reading material that draws attention

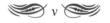

v

to Him and His truth, that reflects His majesty, and that meets the standards of the Holy Scriptures. What this means is that we should take any reading selection to Philippians 4:8 and ask these simple questions: "Is it true? Is it noble? Is it right? Is it pure? Is it lovely? Is it admirable? Is it excellent? Is it praiseworthy?"

As we look at the American readers of days gone by we find that the Biblical standard was followed. Such readers featured the finest British and American authors who emphasized God, morality, the wonders of creation, and respect for one's country.

The Christian Liberty Nature Reader Series follows the pattern of the past. Believing that the student can gain an enhanced appreciation for God by studying His creation (Psalm 19:1; Romans 1:20), this textbook seeks to present the majestic splendor of His handiwork.

It is our prayer that this series will give to the reader the joy that is to be associated with "good reading", and that the knowledge imparted will help "make wise the simple" (Psalm 19:7).

Dr. Paul D. Lindstrom
1939–2002
Founder of Christian Liberty Academy School System

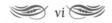

vi

Chapter One
All About Ants

A Look at an Ant

You have been told that an insect is a living creature with a body made in rings and divided into three parts. Most insects have six legs, four wings, and two feelers. There is a great order of insects which we shall call the hook-wing family. The wasp, bee, sawfly, and ant belong to this family. They are the most outstanding of all the insects. They can do many strange and curious things. You will know insects of this great family by their wings. The larger front wings fold back over the smaller rear wings when at rest. In flight, the upper front wings hook firmly to the lower rear ones.

Wasp

If you look carefully at some kinds of insects, you will soon think that what I have told you is not quite true. Why will you think that? You will say to me, "The fly has only two wings, not four; and the ant has no wings at all." Ah, but

Bee

wait until you study about ants and flies and see what you will think then.

The body of an insect is divided into three parts. The first part is its **head** which contains the mouth, eyes, and feelers. The mouth of all the hook-wing insects has two jaws for cutting or for carrying things. The mouth is nearly as wide as the head. Above the mouth are two knobs. These knobs are two big eyes, one on each side of the head. On the top of the head between the two big eyes, there are some little eyes. You see, insects are as well supplied with eyes as crabs are with legs. The back part, or **abdomen**, of the body of many insects is fastened to the middle part, or **thorax**, by a small joint. God created insects in this way because they need to bend, or even double up, to do some of their work.

Fly

The hook-wing family, or order, is divided into two great kinds. The insects of one kind carry a little "saw." The insects of the other kind carry a "sword." The "sword" is a stinger which is used to fight battles or to kill things for food. The "saw" is a blade that is used to cut holes in plants to make nice soft nests or houses for the eggs. Among the "saw" carriers is the fine, long fly, called a **sawfly**. Bees, ants, wasps, and others carry the stinger. If you find one of these insects, you will see all the parts of which I have told you.

Let us first take a look at an ant. The head of an ant seems very large for its body, and its eyes seem very large for the head. They look Ant as if they would be heavy for the little ant to carry. Most ants have very good eyes and can see above ground and underground; but there is one kind of ant that is blind. The jaws of an ant have tiny "teeth" that are often quite worn down in an old worker. Its jaws are well made for digging.

Next to the ant's head is its middle part, or thorax. On the bottom part of the thorax are attached six jointed legs. Its feet, which are also jointed, have small hairs which help the ant run up and down a piece of glass or hang upside down on a wall. Its feet are also made for digging. On the top part of the thorax are attached four wings—two large and two small. The upper pair of wings are larger than the lower ones. But you may argue, "My ant has no wings!" Well, let me tell you a secret. The wings of your ant have been cut off or unhooked, as you shall learn shortly.

Next to the ant's thorax is the end part, or abdomen. The abdomen of an ant's body is made of six rings.

On the tip, or pointed end, of this back part is the stinger.

There are many families of ants. Each family has its own name and its own ways. All ants are clever, so people have often called them "the wise insects." Would you like to learn about their homes, offspring, and way of life? Before you begin, go to your backyard or a nearby field and find an anthill. Remember to take some sugar or bits of cake to feed the ants. Sit by the anthill for an hour, or so. Be careful not to disturb the hill or alarm the ants. Find out all that you can about them. Facts that you learn by observation (watching carefully and noting how things appear, sound, and act) will be remembered more than any other way.

The Life of an Ant

In anthills, we find queen ants, drone ants, and worker ants. The drone ants have no stinger and do no work, but they have wings. Their bodies are longer and more slim than those of the queens'. The queen ants have stingers, and their bodies are round and dark. Queens and newborn ants, who do not go out into the sunshine, have a lighter color. The workers are smaller and darker than the queens and drones, and they do not have any wings. Workers are of two sizes, large and small. They are the builders, nurses, soldiers, and servants of the others.

In an anthill, there may be many queens at one time. A queen ant is not like a queen bee, who allows no other queen to live near her. Queen ants work hard. They are both mothers and queens. Sometimes, they will even act as soldiers. I think that "mother ant" is a better name than "queen ant," because the word "queen" may make you think that this ant rules the rest. This is not so. Ants have no leader and no ruler. God created each ant to act as it should without being told. The main work of the queen ant is to lay eggs. In a short time, out of each egg comes a lively, hungry, little baby ant. It is called a larva.

A larva is like a small, white worm. This little creature needs to be washed, fed, kept warm and dry, and taken into the air and sunshine. It must be cared for, very much as the baby in your home is cared for. The workers, who act as nurses, are very kind to the young larvae. How do they wash these little things? They lick them all over, as the mother cat licks her kittens. They use such care that they keep them nearly as white as snow. The nurses feed the baby ants four or five times each day. They prepare the food in their crops, to make it soft and fit for the little ants. The nurses also stroke and smooth the larvae. It seems as if they pat and pet them. When the weather is cold, they keep the larvae indoors. When it is warm and dry, they hurry to carry them up to the top of the hill. They place them there to **bask** in the sun. If any rain comes, or the hill is broken, the nurses run to carry the babies to a safe place.

When the larva is full grown, it spins around itself a little fine net, which wraps it all up. When people see these white bundles in the anthills, they call them "ant eggs." They are not eggs but pupa cases, or **cocoons**. In them, the ants are getting ready to  come out, with legs and wings, as full-grown ants. The pupa cases come in several sizes. The largest ones are for the queens and drones. The next size holds large workers; the smallest cases hold the smallest workers. In the hills, there are often very tiny ants

Pupa Stage

called **dwarf ants**. When you study more about ants in other books, you can learn about these dwarfs.

After the ants have been in the little cases for some time, they are ready to come out. The nurse ants help them to get free. Many hundreds come out of the cases. They crowd the old home so full that they can scarcely find room to move about. Then they see the light shine in at the little gates on the top of the hill. They feel the warmth of the sun and crawl up and out. They push upon each other. The hill is not wide and high enough for so many uncles, cousins, sisters, and brothers. They act like great crowds in the streets at a big parade, each one struggling for his own place.

Young ants, like young people, wish to set up new homes for themselves. They spread their fine wings and off they fly! Since there is no room in the old hill, they will build a new one. They swarm as the bees do. As they rise high from the earth, they drift off on the wind. Many of them tire out and die, and others are blown into the water and are drowned. A few live and settle on places fit for a new anthill.

It is the mother or queen ant who chooses the new home. When she has found the right place, what do you think she does? She takes off her wings, as she does not care to fly any more. The queen does not tear off her wings. She unhooks them and lets them fall away, and she does not seem to miss them.

The Ant's Home

Ants live in nests made in the earth. We call them anthills because, above the ground, they are shaped like hills. It is the queen ants who begin to build the anthills. Like mother wasps, mother ants work on their nests until enough ants grow up to do all the work. After that, like queen bees, they do no work; but the worker ants will not allow them to go from home.

When the mother, or queen, ant finds a place for her new home, what does she do first? Mrs. Ant takes off her wings because they would be in her way while she works. She presses the edge

of a wing upon the ground, pushing it up and loosening the hook, just as you may unhook a dress. Then she begins to dig. At first, Mrs. Ant acts much like a dog does when it digs after a chipmunk or a rabbit. She lays her big head close to the ground, and with her front feet, she digs up the soil and tosses it back between her hind legs.

Mrs. Ant digs as her cousin, Mrs. Wasp, digs. She keeps waving her little feelers, as if to find out the kind of soil. Soon she has a hole deep enough to cover her body. It is too deep for her to throw out the dirt with her feet. Now she uses her feet and her jaws to dig with, as well. Where the soil is sandy, Mrs. Ant takes it out grain by grain. At first, she must back out of her hole. Soon her hallway is so wide that she can turn about after she has backed a few steps.

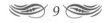

As she continues to make the hall, Mrs. Ant bites off bits of dirt with her jaws and rolls them up with her feet. Then she uses the back part of her body to press and push the earth into firm balls. These balls are carried out and laid by the door. Slowly, layer by layer, these balls form the anthill. When the hall is two or three inches long, she makes a room for her babies. Soon Mrs. Ant has many helpers. Then they make more halls and more rooms for eggs, larvae, pupae, and food.

To make a room, the ants often have to stand on their back legs and bite the earth off, as they reach up their heads. Sometimes they lie on their sides to clean off or smooth the side wall. They have even been seen lying on their backs, as men do when they work on their cars. An anthill is made of many little rooms— some are connected to other rooms and some are not. There are bedrooms, nurseries, pantries, and dining rooms. Many of the rooms are shaped like a horseshoe, but some are round. The ants press and knead the floors and walls to make them hard and smooth. Sometimes they line the walls with a sticky soil, like paste, to keep the earth from falling in. Some ants seem to make a kind of glue, or **varnish**, with which they line their walls.

We can learn a lot about how to live together from the ants. Ants are very kind to each other in their work. If they push or step on each other in haste, they never fight about it. They also know how to work and how to rest. After a little hard work, they stop, clean their bodies, take some food, and sleep. As Proverbs 6:6–8 says, "Go to the ant, you sluggard! Consider her ways and be wise, which, having no captain, overseer or ruler, provides her supplies in the summer, and gathers her food in the harvest." All of us would do well to heed this command lest poverty come upon us like a bandit or shortage like an armed man (Proverbs 6:2).

Now I will tell you about a very unusual anthill. It was made by big black ants in a little valley between two hills of sand. A very large sheet of thick paper had blown into this

valley. The paper had been around a piece of ham and was very greasy. It had lain on the ground crumpled up in sun, snow, and rain for a year. By that time, it was hard and stiff and weeds had grown up about it. One day, as I was going by, I saw ants running in and out of the folds of the paper. I took a stick and turned the top fold open like a lid. It was full of ants and of white pupa cases, cocoons. The ants, I think, liked the folds of the paper for halls, and the larger wrinkles for rooms. They had found out how to have a house without much work in making it. When I opened this paper hill, they ran in swarms to pick up the white bundles. Poor things! They did not know where to go for safety. So I laid the lid of their house back in its place, and soon they were quiet again.

The Ants at Home

We have taken a look at the ants and have seen how their hill is made. Now let us see how they live in their hill home. When we go to visit the ants, we shall find some of them running all about the hill and in the halls. These are the worker ants. Others seem to stand on the hill like soldiers, watching for any danger that may come near. If you look closely, maybe you will see them defend their home.

When the drones and the queens are young, the worker ants let them go out and fly. When they go out, the drones seldom come back because they become lost or die. Some of the young queens, however, come back—except for those who go off to make new hills. When the young queens settle down to their work of laying eggs, the worker ants do not let them leave the hill anymore. How do they keep the queens in, though? If the queens have not taken off their pretty wings, the workers will take them off and throw them away! If the queens try to walk off, the worker ants will pick them up in their jaws and carry them back.

The ants are very kind to their queens. They feed them and pet them, so they become very lazy. They do not even care to lay their eggs in a nice, clean place; they drop their eggs anywhere. The kind worker ants pick the eggs up and take them to a soft bedroom. When there are too many young queens in one hill, they do not have a war, as the bees do. The workers settle the trouble by taking off the wings of some of the young queens and turning them into worker ants. This is done before the queens begin to lay eggs.

How do the weather and seasons affect the ants? In cold, wet weather the ants stay at home. If it starts to rain when they are out, the ants hurry back. Early

in the day and late in the afternoon, they all seem to be very busy. In the hot hours of the day, especially during summer, they stay in the hill and rest. In the spring, however, I have seen very large swarms of ants busily working about their hill when the weather was warm and dry. In very hot lands, the ants build hills that stay cool even when the hot sun shines down on them. Some of these hills are taller than you. They also work hard all winter to store up food, as you will learn shortly. In cooler lands, however, the ants are "asleep," or **torpid**, during the winter. In autumn, the young swarms of ants usually go out to start new **colonies**.

What do ants like to eat? Best of all, ants like sugar and **nectar**. They get nectar from flowers, and in other ways of which I will soon tell you. Some like seeds that have a sweet taste. For this reason they eat some kinds of grass seeds, oats, apple seeds, and such things.

Ants take their food by licking it. Their little rough tongues wear away bits of seed; they also suck up the oil and juice of seeds. They seem to press the food with their jaws. It has been found out that they know how to moisten their food and make it soft. If you give them dry sugar or cake, they turn it into a kind of paste or "honey." Then it is easier for them to suck or drink it up.

If you put a nest of ants with plenty of earth into a large glass jar and put some food near by for the ants to eat, they may settle down in the jar and make a home. If you cover the outside of the jar with thick, dark paper, the ants may build close to the glass. Then, when you take off the paper, you will be able to see the halls and storerooms. You might put such a jar in a safe place outdoors. Then you would be able to study the ants, as they roam around nearby or do their work inside the jar. In this way, you can learn a lot about ants as you watch them live and work.

The Ants on a Trip

The round hole in the anthill is called the "gate." The ants can close it with a bit of stone. Often there are

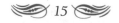

two, three, or even more, gates for one anthill. Once
I saw a hill with six large gates.

Now I will tell you how ants move from one house to
another. One day I saw a line of ants moving all one
way by my garden path. They were black ants. They
went two by two, or one and two, close to each other.
Every one had in its jaws a white bundle. I found that
they all came from an anthill. They came up out of
the gate very fast, one by one, each with its bundle.
About two or three inches from this line of ants I saw
another line. This line went to the hill, not from it.
They went in good order. They had no bundles when
they went into the hill; when they came out, each
had a bundle, and joined the other line of ants.

I went along with the stream of ants that had the
white bundles. I found that they went to a new hill,
about thirty feet from the old hill. There they laid
down their bundles, and went back to the old hill
to bring more. The bundles lay heaped in a ring all
about the gate of the new city. Out of this gate ran
other ants in haste. They caught up the bundles, one
by one, and carried them in. In about half an hour
they were nearly all taken in, and the ants brought
no more. The moving was over.

With a long blade of grass, I gently took up a few
bundles. I hid them behind a stone, some six inches

off. When all the rest of the bundles left at the hill were carried in, the ants went down the gates. But in a minute out came three or four ants. They ran about wildly and searched the ground. They went in circles and looked over the ground with much care. The circles grew wider. At last one came up behind the stone and found the bundles. The ant picked up one bundle and ran. Then this ant met the other ants and, I think, told them the news. For at once the other ants ran up to the stone, and each took up a bundle. Then they all ran into the hill. Can ants count? It looked as if they knew how many bundles they had. It also looked as if they knew that two ants must go for two bundles.

A man who took bundles from a march, in the same way I did, thinks that the

ants smell the hidden bundles. He says they will not search for the bundles if you hide them in the earth.

The Farmer Ants

You have heard about the spider which makes a den in the ground. It puts a trapdoor on its den and plants ferns on the door to hide it. The spider becomes a gardener in this way, and all its plants grow well. There is an ant that also becomes a gardener, or farmer. This ant lives on its "farm" in warm places around the world. In the United States, they are found in Texas, Florida, and in one or two other warm states. These farmer ants raise grain to eat. The grain is a kind of grass with a large seed. Some people call it "ant rice."

The farmer ants do not live in a small hill that is as big as your hand but in a large hill that is sometimes flat and sometimes high. It is often as wide as a big room that is in the shape of a circle. In this circle, all the weeds and all kinds of grass are cut down, except for the one kind of grass which the ants like. The earth inside the circle is kept clean and smooth. Only the seeds of the "ant rice" are left to grow. When the "ant rice" is ripe, the ants pick up the seeds as they fall to the ground and take them into the hill to special storerooms. After all the seeds have fallen, the ants cut down the old stems and take them away. The circle is then clean for the next crop.

It is most likely that, as the farmer ants let this "ant rice" grow on their hill, it sows itself by its fallen seed. Still the ants are real farmers, as they keep their land clean, tend and gather the crop, and store it up. The ants watch the stored seeds and, after it rains, carry them out to dry in the sun. They know that, if the seeds are left wet, they will sprout and grow. Some ants also cut the seeds so they will not sprout. The way God created these little insects to plant, raise, harvest, and store their food shows how wise He is.

If the farmer ants run out of seeds, they will go a long way from their hill to find new seeds to bring home. They like to go where horses have eaten, for there they find scattered oats. In some places, they carry off a lot of grain from the fields. In Florida, there is one kind of ant that climbs the stalk of the millet plant, cuts off the seeds, and carries them home. When ants take seeds to their hill, they husk and clean them and throw the bad seeds away.

These ants like to eat the seeds that they gather. They also feed them to their young. How do the ants eat the hard grain? Their tongues are like files, or something like that of the little shellfish called the drill. The ants can rasp, file, and press the grain, so they can lick up the oil and juice of the seeds. One kind of ant in Florida rolls up the dust, or pollen, of pine cones into little balls and stores them up to eat. Another kind of ant in New Jersey cuts new, little pine trees into tiny pieces, just as these **saplings** break through the ground, and carries them to the nest to eat.

Did you ever see the ants which like sunflower seeds to eat? They are large ants, and when they have climbed onto the disk of a sunflower plant, they pull out the ripe seeds and carry them away. It is said that these ants plant the sunflower seeds in a ring around their hill. Since they have not been seen to plant the seeds, we may not be quite sure that they do so. Perhaps they build where they see young sunflower plants growing. Yet it is possible that ants plant seeds of some kind. You see, there are still many things left for you to discover in God's creation. It will be well for you to keep your eyes open.

Ants and Their Trades

Since you know that bees, ants, and wasps all belong to the same great family of living creatures, you will not wonder that many of their ways are alike. You may have read how, in the spring, Mrs. Social Wasp builds her home and raises a **brood** of babies. These, as soon as they are full-grown, begin to build more rooms and nurse the new babies that come along. Mrs. Ant does as Mrs. Wasp does. Mrs. Ant begins a new hill, and as her children grow, they help her build. She does not often begin her hill in the spring, though. Mrs. Ant chooses the early fall to build her hill. As the eggs change into worker ants, Mrs. Ant gets plenty of help in her work.

You have seen bees swarm and hang in a bunch on the branch of a tree. Ants also cling together and form balls, but they do this for warmth or safety. It is called "snugging." In some lands, in times of flood, ants form balls as large as your soccer ball. In this way, they can float on the water so they will not drown.

As Mrs. Wasp makes paper, Mrs. Ant can also make a thin paper for her nest. It is poor paper, however, compared to the paper Mrs. Wasp makes. Mrs. Wasp is the best of the paper-makers. Likewise, as Mrs. Bee cuts leaves to line her nest, Mrs. Ant sometimes does the same thing. With the cut leaves she lines her neat, little nest.

There is a brown ant that is a mason. It makes its nest of little balls of mud, laid up like bricks in a wall. Then there is a carpenter ant, just as there is a carpenter bee. These carpenters cut their way into trees and logs. They hollow out the inside of a tree, or beam, until it is ready to fall to pieces. In this way they do much harm.

Although spiders are not insects, some have ways which are similar to the ways of certain ants. As the spider makes a fine spun ball to put her babies in, there is an ant that makes a woolly nest. Probably you have also read of the **tower spider** that builds a neat tower of sticks, straw, and grass over its nest. There is an ant that thatches its hill in much the same way.

Besides their other trades, the ants know the trade of war. Ants are usually mild and kind to each other while at work, but soldier ants are brave and are ready to do battle. When it comes to war, it is interesting to see how much ant ways are like human ways. The ants make war to get slaves, or servants. They also make war to get cows, as you will learn shortly. They seem to have some other reasons for war, as well. When the ant army marches, it keeps in line and in order. It seems to have captains to rule and lead it. Scouts go before the army to seek out the way. The anthill also has some soldiers which act like sentries, to see that no danger comes near. When a worker ant gets into trouble, it will run to a soldier for help.

The soldier ants have very large heads, as if they wear big hats. Some of them have smooth heads, and others have hairy heads. They eat a lot and love to sleep. These soldier ants do not do much work, except when they awaken for battle. In an anthill, the soldiers are larger and often more in number than the other ants. In a battle, two soldier ants will often cling to each other by their jaws, until both die. The usual way in which an ant soldier kills a foe is by cutting off the head. Sometimes the battle ends without any killing. At other times, the ants are very fierce, and large numbers are cut to pieces.

When strange ants get into a hill, sometimes they are driven out; sometimes they are killed; sometimes they are treated kindly. One time, I put a black ant into the gate of a city of brown ants. You should have seen how they drove it out! The black ant ran as if it were wild with fear. Three or four brown ants chased it to the edge of their hill.

Though some strange ants are cast out so fiercely, there are two or three kinds of beetles which go into anthills and live with the ants. The ants do not harm them in any way. You shall hear about that when we have some stories about beetles.

The Slave Ants

Now I must tell you about the slave ants and their owners. The main family of the slave-making ants is called "the shining," because their bodies shine with a gloss like varnish. The slave-making ants and their slaves are found in many parts of the world. The masters are of a bright, glossy light-brown or red color, but the slave ants are dark-brown or black. The slave-owning ants walk about their hill in an idle way. These masters do not build their houses, nurse their babies, or feed themselves. Often they do not even brush and clean their own bodies. They leave all these duties to their slaves. The masters only make war and steal slaves or slave babies. The slave ants do all the work. If a war rises, however, they also fight for the hill and their owners.

The army of the slave-makers marches to the hill of a tribe of ants which they wish to seize as slaves. They carry off the pupa cases, in which little new ants are getting legs and wings. These are taken to the hill of the owners and brought up with their own young. No slave-ant eggs are laid in the masters' hill, for the queens lay all the eggs, and the queens are not slaves. The slaves are stolen when they are eggs, larvae, or pupae. The owners seem to be very kind to their little slaves, and as the slaves grow up and fill the hill, they seem to do very much as they please.

Ants will now and then change their home, leaving their old hill and making a new one. When they do

this, if some of the ants do not seem ready to leave the old hill, the others drag them off by force. The slaves build the new hills and take their owners to live in the new home. If a queen ant tries to wander off her hill, her slaves drag her back. If she does not wish to move to her new home, her slaves carry her off all the same.

When the master ants are ready to make a move, the slaves pick them up and carry them away. How can they do that? The ants carry all burdens in their jaws. The slave and the master lock their jaws, the owner curls up the back of its body, and the slave carries it off. The grip of an ant's jaw is very strong. It can carry things much larger than its own body.

Other ants can also carry objects larger than themselves. There is the ant which uses the pine needles for food. It carries the bits of pine laid over its back much as a man carries a gun. There is a little groove in this ant's head, where the bits of pine rest. I have seen very large hills covered with carefully cut bits of pine needles. I think they have been sucked dry and then cast out.

There is another kind of ant called the "parasol ant," because it cuts off tiny bits of leaf and carries them over its head like a **parasol**. An army of this kind on the march looks very funny. These ants line their nests with the bits of leaf to keep the dirt from falling in. These parasol ants are very large and their nests cover a large space. The bits of leaf are cut about the size of a dime. The ants carry them in their jaws, each piece by a little end left for a stem. Some parasol ants live in Florida and Texas, and many others are found in South America.

Wonder Ants

Now you must hear about the ants that keep "cows." I have told you that ants like "honey." These **honey ants** take all their food by lapping and sucking it. They suck nectar from flowers. If you look at the plants in the garden or house, you may see on the leaves some very small green things that seem to eat the leaves. Your mother will tell you these are "plant lice," and that they spoil her plants. The name of this little insect is **aphid**. That is a very pretty name. The aphid is very small, and is often of the color of the leaf it feeds on. This tiny thing can make "honey" in its body much as bees do, but the aphid does not store up the "honey"; it drops it on the leaf as it feeds. This is called **honeydew**. The honey ants eat the honeydew from the leaves, and they know that it comes from the aphid. They stroke and tap the aphid with their feelers so that more honeydew will fall.

The honey ants go from one aphid to another, until they get all the honey they want. The ants can carry home the honeydew, and give it to other ants. The nurse ants will carry it to the baby ants. The  workers take it to the queens, owners, and soldiers. The aphid is called the ant's "cow." A hill of ants will seem to own a herd of these tiny green "cows." They go to them on their leaf, and get the honeydew. They know and claim their own "cows." It is just like having a herd of cows in pasture, as the farmer does. You know that people often keep cows in stables and feed them there; the honey ant does the same thing. There is a kind of aphid that loves the dark and feeds on roots. Some ants keep a herd of these hidden in the ground. They pet, stroke, and clean them to get their honeydew.

Honey ants have been seen to fight for days over a herd of aphid "cows." One hill of ants had no "cows," and they tried to steal the "cows" that belonged to another hill. After four days, the lady who watched them got twenty aphids and gave them to the hill that had none. Then the war ended. The honey ants which got the new "cows" seemed very glad. They licked and petted the aphids and put them in a safe place. They took honeydew from them and fed the soldiers. This seems just like a fairy tale, but it is quite true. All these things can be seen if you look out for them, but you must be patient and anxious to learn.

In warm summer days, when your mother tells you that it is too hot to run about much, what will you do? Why not make a tent of an umbrella, placed near an anthill, and watch these pretty, curious little creatures?

The Ways of Ants

I have told you that ants like nectar and sweets. They will also suck the juices and soft parts of many other kinds of food. Some ants eat nearly everything that can be eaten. Almost all ants will eat other insects and suck the eggs or pupae of other insects. This habit makes ants very useful. Certain worms and bugs that destroy orange trees and cotton plants are killed by ants. Ants also eat other insects that annoy men. If a coat that is covered with these pesky insects is laid near an anthill, the ants will have made it quite clean in an hour or two.

You have seen the cat clean its fur coat with its paws and tongue. The ant washes or brushes itself in much the same way as that of the cat. The ant is very neat

and clean in its habits.
It takes many naps in
a day, and after each
nap it brushes itself. It
also brushes itself after
working and eating. On
its foreleg, the ant has a
little comb shaped like
your thumb. With this
it strokes and combs
all dust and dirt from
its body. Then it draws
its front foot through its
mouth to clean the comb
and to make it moist, so
that it will do its work
well. The ant has also little
brushes on its other feet;
so you see there is no reason
why it should not keep itself very
trim and tidy.

Ants are also very neat about their
nests. They carry out all husks of grain and seeds
and all dead bodies. They carry these far off their
hill. I knew of an ant nest that had been set on a post
in water. It was kept clean by the ants. They soon
learned to drop all refuse over into the water.

Ants bury their dead. When an ant dies, some of the other ants pick up the body to carry it off and bury it. They do not like to put dead bodies near their hill. The ants will carry the dead ones round and round, till they find a good place for them. A lady who spent much time in the study of ants said that the slave-owning ants do not bury the slaves with the masters. They put the dead slaves in one place and the owners in another.

Ants have a stinger, but they seldom use it if they are left alone. Some ants have very sharp ones. The stinger is on the back part of the ant's body. Their stinger is made in three parts. There is a sac for poison, the needle which gives the prick, and the case in which the needle or prickle is kept. This light-colored needle is like a little thorn. With its jaws, the ant grabs the thing it wishes to sting. Then it lifts its body up on its back legs and swings its stinger under, so that it can drive the stinger into the place held by the jaws. The stinger does not do much harm to people, but it will no doubt kill ants and other insects.

Ants also make a kind of juice called "ant acid." They can throw this about when the hill is disturbed. This **acid** must be pretty strong. It will make a dog sneeze and rub his nose. The ants use this acid to keep dogs, mice, beetles, and such creatures away from the anthill.

I have told you that some ants harm trees and plants by gnawing or cutting them. It is only fair now to tell you that some ants help plants to grow. When they creep into flowers for nectar, pollen sticks to their bodies and is carried from one flower to another.

In this way, the ants help the flowers, which in their turn give food to the ants. Of course, the ants do not know what they are doing for the flowers, as bees do not. In God's great plan, however, the ants and bees carry the pollen from flower to flower, helping them to produce seeds and fruit.

These stories about the ants contain only a few of the many wonderful things that can be said about this insect. I hope you will like the study of ants well enough to get other books about them and watch ants for yourselves.

Review

1. Describe an insect. How are the wings of hook-winged insects fastened together in flight?

2. Describe an ant. What is the difference between a queen, drone, and worker ant?

3. What is meant by "queen ant"? What becomes of the queen ant's wings?

4. How is an anthill begun?   Describe an anthill. What is the opening of an anthill called?

5. How do ants move from one hill to another?

6. How do nurse ants care for baby ants?

7. What can you say about soldier ants?

8. How do certain ants make slaves?

9. What insect is called the "ant's cow"? Describe the ants and their cows.

10. How does the ant clean its body?

11. What do you know about farmer ants? About parasol ants?

12. What kinds of food do ants eat? How do ants eat?

13. How do ants bury their dead?

14. Describe the march of an ant army.

15. What do you know about "ant acid"?

16. How do ants treat each other while they are at work?

17. What becomes of ants during winter in cold countries? In spring, when it rains? In summer, when it is hot out? In autumn?

18. Of what use are ants? How do ants carry things?

19. How can you study ants for yourselves?

Chapter Two
All About Flies

A Look at a Housefly

Look at a worm crawling about on the earth. Then look at a fly with its dark, blue-green body and thin wings. See how it whirls in the air! You might say, "These two are not at all alike." Yet there is one time in a fly's life when it is very much like a worm. For this reason, some people set flies and worms next to each other when they study them.

As soon as you look at a fly, you know that it is an insect. You have learned that an insect usually has four wings, although it may have two wings; six legs; a body that is divided into three parts; and a pair of feelers, or **antennae**, which are like horns. An insect also breathes through all its body and not by lungs as you do. It has a row of holes in each of its sides through which it breathes. In addition, the life of an insect passes through the following three stages: the egg stage; grub, or larva, stage; and pupa stage. When it is in the **pupa** it gets legs and wings. Do you know what pupa means? It means "baby" or "doll."

There are some kinds of insects that vary in some of these points, and the fly is one of them. If you look at a fly, you will see that it has only two wings, not four; therefore, it is not one of the hook-wings. Many insects can fold their wings, but the fly cannot fold its wings, so it lays them back over its body.

Let us first look at a fly when it is most like an earthworm. First of all, the fly comes from a tiny egg laid by the mother fly. When the egg opens, the baby fly is not like a fly, but like a little earthworm, both in its looks and in the way in which it is made. It is a small white grub with rings, and on the rings are hooks.

Fly Eggs

If you want to watch fly eggs change into grubs, lay a bit of meat in the sun on a hot day. Soon flies will lay their eggs on it. These small, white eggs are put on the meat as if they had been planted. The next day these eggs will turn into grubs which grow very fast. The grub of the fly has a pair of jaws like hooks. It also has two little dots which will become eyes when it becomes an adult fly. In regard to its hooked jaws and eye-points, the grub of a fly is not like an earthworm. The fly grub eats and grows, then its skin gets tough and hard and forms a little case, called a **cocoon**, in the shape of a barrel. It closes in the grub, as if in a coffin. Now the young fly seems to be dead, but it is only resting. As it rests, the grub turns into a creature that has wings and legs; soon it will be able to fly and walk. As the fly lies in its cocoon, first the legs and then the wings grow. It also gets a head with a mouth, eyes, and "trunk." As you will see, it turns from a grub into an amazing insect. In its little cocoon, however, it is tightly closed up, so its legs and wings are all bent up. In a few days the change will be complete, and it will be ready to come out.

At just the right time, it moves and pulls and tries to get free from its hard case. It strikes the end of the cocoon with its head time after time. At last it breaks the cocoon open, and out comes the fly! It stands in the air and in the sun, if it can, and shakes itself. The fly is cold and weak; but the air soon dries its wings and blows out the wrinkles. In a very few minutes the fly is strong and happy. Then it spreads its wings and sails off to look for something good to eat and to enjoy its life.

How to Look at a Fly

Do you think a fly is a very small and common thing? Is it worth looking at? Let us see about that. First, there is its head with two great eyes; we will look at its eyes shortly, and then you will see how curious they are. Besides its big eyes, the fly has three little eyes which are set on the top of its head. On the front of its head, it also has a "trunk," or tube, and a pair of feelers, or antennae. Inside the head is the fly's brain, which is very much like that of a worm's. It is only a tiny white dot.

Next, behind the head is the fly's chest. The head has the shape of half of an egg laid sidewise, but the chest is nearly square. It is made of three rings. On the first ring is a pair of legs. On the next ring is a pair of legs and a pair of wings. On the last ring is a pair of legs, and near these legs are two little clubs covered with fine hair. The fly uses these clubs to halt or to balance on its wings. They help the fly like the second pair of wings helps other insects. The third part of a fly's body is the largest. It is egg-shaped and joins the chest by the thick end. This part also is made of rings.

Now let us look more closely at the head of a fly. The feelers, or antennae, are like two long, fine **plumes** made in joints. The fly uses these antennae to feel, or **sense**, things near it. Some people think that flies smell and hear with these feelers; but they are so fine that a breath can jar them, and the fly might seem to hear when it only feels. This is the same for students who cannot hear; they can "hear" when someone raps on the floor. They do not hear the noise, but they feel the **vibration**, and answer as if they could hear.

Let us look at the mouth of the fly. The lip of a fly runs out into a long, slim tube. With this, it sucks up its food. At the end of this tube is a little flat plate. Close by it are two sharp hairs. These are to prick the food, so that the tube can suck it more easily. When the fly is not eating, it can close up this tube, like a telescope, to keep it safe.

The main parts to notice in a fly's head are its eyes. These are so large that they make up nearly all the head. These big, bright eyes look as if they had varnish 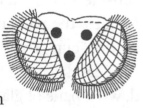 on them. Now each of these eyes is made up of a very great many small eyes. There are four thousand of these small eyes. Between these two big eyes are three little single eyes, set in this way. Wise people have studied the eyes of flies for many years, and do not yet know all about them. You see, even in a fly there is much left for some of you to find out.

Let us now look at the middle part, or **thorax**, of a fly. The fly's wings are attached to the second ring of the thorax. These wings have a fine, thin, clear covering which is held out on a tiny frame, like a network. The fly moves its wings very quickly; the motion of its wings is what makes the fly's buzzing sound. Now we come to the legs of our fly. One pair of legs is attached to each of the three rings of the thorax, and each leg is made in five joints. The "foot" of a fly also has five joints. The last joint of the "foot" has two claws and a little pad. The legs and feet are covered with fine hairs. The hairs catch on little points or rough edges. Thus the fly can walk, as you would say, "upside down," and does not fall. Besides, the pad and hairs act like a

Fly Foot

suction cup. They suck air from under the foot, so they can keep the fly from falling as he runs up and down a pane of glass.

Mrs. Fly and Her Babies

I suppose you have heard your mother say, "I wish there were not so many flies!" The fact is, flies cause us a lot of trouble. Their noise tires and annoys most people. Flies also lay their eggs in and on food, which spoils it. Moreover, they cover our clean walls and glass with small black spots. Can you believe that just one fly can be the mother of two million baby flies in just one year? Many insects die soon after laying eggs. Bees and wasps do not, nor do flies. Bees and wasps take care of their eggs and their young, but the fly mother does not.

Mrs. Fly has more than a hundred eggs to lay at one time. It is quite plain she could not take care of so many babies. She must let them all look out for themselves. Still, Mrs. Fly shows much sense as to where she puts her eggs. She finds a place where they will be likely to find food and grow. If the place is too wet, the baby flies would drown when they leave their eggs. If the place is too dry, they would wither up and die. Mrs. Fly does not lay her eggs on a stone or a piece of wood; she lays them in some kind of soft food. Mrs. Fly can live all summer if she is able, but the cold will kill her; even a frosty day will kill her. A few flies, however, hide and live over winter in a sleepy, or **torpid**, state. When spring comes, they come out to raise new swarms.

Birds, spiders, wasps, cats, dogs, and some other animals like to eat flies. These creatures kill flies by the millions. People also kill flies with poison and fly traps. If so many were not killed, we should be overrun with them.

In the southern part of North America, there is a plant with a leaf that looks like a jug. On the seam of its leaf hang drops of "honey." This juice can make the flies drunk. Flies like this juice, but as soon as they drink it, they become dizzy and act just like they are drunk. Then they fall into the juglike space of the leaf and soon die. One of these plants can kill many flies in one day, but this plant is not the only enemy of flies. Many of our best birds live on flies, and if our birds were all dead we should have much greater trouble with the flies.

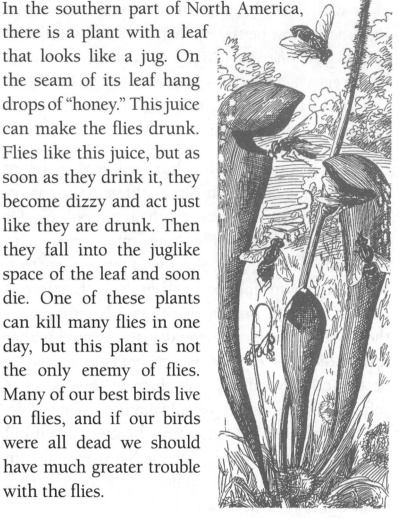

In the autumn you will see flies sitting about as if they feel dull and ill. If you look carefully you will see that the back part of the body is covered with a white dust which looks like corn meal or **mold**. Soon the fly dies. This white dust is a disease that makes the fly stiff and spread out. The fly looks like it is alive, but if you touch it, it crumbles to dust. All around such a dead fly you will see a ring of white mold. This is perhaps a real mold, or tiny plant, that fastens on the fly's body. It uses up all the soft parts which kills the fly, leaving only the dry shell. There is another strange thing about this mold. The body of a fly, that dies in this way, is torn or burst open. The fly looks as if this dust or mold grew so large in its body that it burst open.

Of What Use Are Flies?

How often people cry out, "Oh, I wish there were no flies! What is the use of a fly?" But all things that God has made have their uses. And all God's works are worthy of study. You have learned that bees are of great use. Let us see if Mrs. Fly does any good in the world.

Mrs. Fly is of great use to man. She helps keep him in health. Do you think that very strange? People say, "Oh, these dirty flies!" And yet these "dirty flies" help to keep the world clean! Now you know that over all the world, great numbers of animals die each minute, and many of their bodies lie on the ground and decay. Such bodies in decay cause disease and death to men. In winter, and in cold places, such things do not decay so fast nor make bad odors. If

43

such dead things lie about in summer, however, they will poison the air. Soon we would all be ill. The work of Mrs. Fly is to lay many eggs in these dead bodies. In a few hours, these eggs turn to grubs; then these grubs begin to eat as fast as they can. Soon they leave only dry bones, which can do no harm. They change the dead flesh of animals into their own fat, live bodies.

You know that crabs are among the "street cleaners" of the sea, so flies are among the "street cleaners" of the air and land. Did you ever watch flies dart about, here and there, with a flight like hawks? They are eating up small, evil things, too small for us to see, but these things are still big enough to hurt us if we should get them into our lungs. In our homes many bits of food, plants, or other things also drop to the floor or stairs; these things usually decay and mold, making the air foul. The busy and greedy fly, however, drinks up all the soft parts of these things. So we see that these "dirty flies" really do help to clean away much dirt. On the other hand, it is true that flies carry disease on their feet and trunks from place to place; in this way they can do great harm. The fly, however, serves as food for many birds, fish, frogs, and certain insects. Some of these creatures are used as food for people. Others are full of beauty, or are of use to us, each in its own way. Though the fly is often a trouble to us, we find it is not without its uses. If you look at one of these little creatures through a magnifying glass, you will see that it is quite beautiful.

From what you have read in this story, you must not think that all foul smells kill, nor that things that have no bad smell are always safe. There are some gases that have no odor at all, yet are very deadly; but you will learn more about these things as you study God's great creation.

A Swarm of Flies

Have you heard people speak of **swarms** of flies? By a swarm of flies we mean a great number of flies that live fairly near to each other. By a swarm of bees we mean a number of bees that live and work in one place. A swarm of bees divides the work of its hive. It has one queen bee. She is the mother and ruler of the rest; but flies have no one mother, or queen, for whom the rest work, and no home where they live in common. In fact, they have no work, except that each mother fly drops her eggs where it seems best to her. Then she goes off and leaves her children to grow as best they can.

I have said that the fly likes best to place her eggs on a piece of fresh meat. These eggs soon turn to grubs which spoil the meat. To keep the meat from the flies, a wise cook will put a cover over it. Sometimes the cover is made of wire mesh.

"Now," says the cook, "I can keep away that dirty fly."

Mrs. Fly says, however, "Oh, can you, Mrs. Cook? We will see about that."

So Mrs. Fly sits on top of the wire cover. She puts her little egg tube through one of the fine holes in the net and drops egg after egg from the tube. The eggs fall right on the meat, just where Mrs. Fly wishes them to be.

Then the cook cries out, "How ever did that fly get to my meat?"

Is it not strange that Mrs. Fly knows that her egg tube is the right size to go through the mesh of the wire net? How does she know that the eggs will fall on the meat?

Flies do another strange thing. If many flies are in a room, and you begin to chase them with a fly swatter, they hide. They creep into holes and cracks. They hide in curtains. They go behind pictures. After the hunt is over, out they come—one by one! Flies also know how to "play dead." If you hit one and make it fall, it will lie very still and seem to be dead. Then, after a little while, it softly spreads out its legs and its wings. Then it shakes itself. A moment more, off it goes. This manner of making believe to be dead does not belong to flies only. Nearly all insects, and many other animals, pretend to be dead. It is interesting to watch and see how well they do it.

When a fly dies, other flies come to eat up its body. They put their mouth tubes on the dead fly and begin to suck. Soon the body is sucked dry of all its juice and is only an empty shell. If a fly has been dead only a short time and is not stiff, the wings can still be moved. If one wing is gently tipped up, the other will rise too. They move together, as if they were set on a little spring.

Some Unusual Flies

Although flies are useful, they also do harm to people in many ways. The fly you have been reading about is the common housefly. That fly—with its noise, dirt, and spoiling of food by laying eggs in it—is bad enough. Yet the housefly makes the least trouble of any of its kind. There are many other kinds of flies that are more bothersome. To the family of flies belong gnats, midges, mosquitoes, and crane flies with their long legs. You know well how some of these creatures sting, or—as you may say—"bite."

Let us look at some of these bothersome flies. The **crane fly** hurts the grass lands with its grubs, which spoil grass roots and the shoots of plants. The **gallfly** bites trees and lays its eggs in twigs; then round balls called "galls" grow over the eggs

Gallfly

upon the twigs. These galls injure the trees. There is also the **botfly**, which lays its eggs on the hide of the horse. These eggs cause the skin of the horse to itch. When the horse licks its itchy skin, the eggs go into the bloodstream and finally to the stomach. Then the grubs hatch and eat holes in the stomach of the horse, which make it sick. The farmer will say that his horse is sick with "bots." In Africa, there are flies that kill horses and oxen by biting them. Their bite poisons the cattle and causes fever. Furthermore,

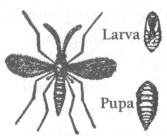
Larva
Pupa
Hessian Fly

farmers will tell you of a very bad fly that spoils wheat and other grain; it is called the **Hessian fly**. There is also a large, handsome, bright green fly which bites horses and annoys them, but does not harm them; it is called the **horsefly**. In some lands, a small **sandfly** causes sore eyes. Flies, as they flit from place to place, sometimes carry with them the suffering of disease, as of sores and ulcers; thus they spread these troubles among people.

Nevertheless, flies—as they go to flowers for nectar—carry the dust of the flowers from one to another. This helps new flowers to grow. There are also some dead flies worth a great deal of money. How is that? These are flies in **amber**. Amber is clear, hard resin which comes from evergreen trees and is bright yellow in color. Sometimes we may see perfect flies, held in clear, light masses of amber. These are used for jewelry. How did they get there? The amber was once a soft gum and the fly landed on it. It stuck fast, and the amber flowed over it and grew hard, burying the fly in a clear, golden tomb. A piece of amber with a fly in it will bring a high price.

The **Spanish fly** is a large, blue-green beetle. Some people think this handsome insect is most useful when it is dead; they use it as a cure for sores. It makes blisters on the skin, which are painful; but even pain can be useful. The blister, though it hurts us, may help in the healing of certain sores. It cures what might be a worse pain. The Spanish fly is not a fly at all! It is a beetle which has been given a fly's name. It is put here at the end of the chapter on flies, because in the next chapter you will read about beetles.

Review

1. How many wings does a fly have? Instead of a second pair of wings, what does it have?

2. Describe a fly's mouth. Does a fly chew or suck its food? What things does a fly eat?

3. Do flies have queens or live in swarms, as bees do?

4. How does a mother fly care for her eggs or her young? Where does she place her eggs?

5. What are the changes a fly goes through from an egg to a full-grown adult? How does the fly come from the pupa case?

6. Describe a fly's feet. How can a fly run up a pane of glass or walk on a ceiling?

7. Why do people dislike flies? How does the fly make its buzzing sound?

8. Name some different kinds of flies. What are some of their unusual ways?

9. What do flies do during cold weather? What do we mean by a swarm of flies?

10. Of what use are flies? What harm do flies do? What are some of the fly's enemies?

11. What is a fly in amber? Is a Spanish fly a true fly? Of what use is it?

Chapter Three
All About Beetles

Clad in Armor

Ladybug or Ladybird Beetle

The next time you go to a flower garden or park, and after a little search, you will find one of the wonders of the world. You will find a small, tough, shiny, red thing with black spots on its back. "Why!" you say, "that is only a **ladybug**, or ladybird." Perhaps you have heard the following little rhyme about it.

> Ladybird, ladybird,
> Fly away home!
> Your house is on fire
> And your children will roam.

Yes, it is one of the beetles, and every beetle is a wonder. Come, study these wonders.

The winged insects are divided into two great classes, "eaters" and "drinkers." That is what their Latin names mean. Butterflies, houseflies, bees, and others, are "drinkers." That is, they get their food by sucking it through a pipe or tube. This tube is on the front part of their heads; and it is really their upper lips grown long and round. The other great class, the "eaters," eat their food with their mouths. Some suck or lick food; others use their jaws to crush and break their food.

Beetles belong to the class of "eaters." The beetles are covered with a hard, hornlike shell which is like a case. In this case, they look like soldiers from the Middle Ages who wore armor from head to foot. Beetles belong to the great family of the ring-made creatures. If you find a large, round beetle—with big jaws, feelers, and legs—does it not look a little like Mr. Crab who is also ring-made? Mr. Beetle is a large beetle that likes to live among the grasses and weeds near the seashore. When he and Mr. Crab meet on the sand they may think they are cousins.

Now let us find a beetle and look at it more closely. You will often find dead beetles on the sidewalk or in the grass. You can take them apart and compare them with what you read about them.

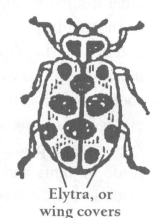

Elytra, or wing covers

The first thing that you will notice in the beetle is the hard wing cases over its back. These wing cases are called **elytra** and look like little shells that have nice hinges to hold them in their place. These two wing covers fit close to each other over the beetle's back. When the beetle flies, it lifts them away from its wings. These cases are used for "armor," not for flying. When you take off these covers, you will see a pair of neatly folded wings lying under the elytra. These wings are made a lot like Mrs. Wasp's. The fine silken underwings are the pair with which beetles fly. Some beetles do not have this second pair of wings, so they cannot fly; they creep from place to place. Other beetles have an upper pair of wings so short that they do not half cover their bodies.

Watch a beetle as it crawls on the ground. Now look at it! When its back flies open, two bright-colored cases rise up. This crawling thing sweeps into the air on a pair of wide thin wings! The part of the beetle's body that is under the wings has rings like those of the wasp. Its body is divided into three parts like other insects. Its four wings and six legs are fastened on the middle part, or **thorax**. The two wings that are fastened on the upper part of the beetle's thorax fold down over its **abdomen**. At the end of the female's abdomen is a part called the ovipositor, or "egg-placer." With the **ovipositor**, Mrs. Beetle lays her eggs in a safe place. The legs and feet of the beetle are made in joints and have hairs on them. Its legs are made in such a way that they cannot spread out as far as those of a spider, wasp, or fly.

Now here is Mr. Beetle's **head**. It has two jaws, two feelers, a mouth, and eyes. There is a little, hornlike shield over the mouth. In fact, the whole beetle is in a snug, hornlike coat. We may call this coat a "suit of armor." The eyes of the beetle are like those of the fly. Very many eyes are set in what seem to be two large **compound eyes**; however, the beetle does not have three **single eyes** on the top of its head. Sometimes he has two small simple eyes at the back of his head. The splendid colors of the beetle are on its hornlike coat. The other night, I caught a beetle which had the under part of its chest, or thorax, covered with hairs that look like velvet. It seemed to have on a rich brown velvet vest.

When Mr. Beetle Was Young

In stories about the ant, fly, wasp, and bee, you have learned that young insects go through three changes—this is called **metamorphosis**. First there is a small, white or light-colored **egg**; then a fat, greedy **larva**; then a **pupa**. The insects you have heard about so far pass through all these changes in a short time. Some of the young beetles also do this; but there are some beetles which spend one, two, or three years—even more—as eggs and grubs. Most of the insects you have learned about live a long time after they get their wings, but those beetles that live a long time as grubs live a short time after they get their wings.

You will not care to hear about beetles while they are only eggs. As eggs, they lie quiet where the mother beetle hid them. These eggs are placed in earth or in water. Some kinds of beetles put their eggs into the bodies of dead animals, others into holes in trees, and still others into fruit. After a while, the larvae come out. Sometime you may find long, soft, white "worms," with their bodies divided into rings. They have two big eyes; two jaws; no feet—or, perhaps, very small ones; and never any wings. Would you guess they are Mrs. Beetle's children? By and by, they will have strong wings; long, strong legs; hornlike bodies; and, very often, colors like a rainbow.

The white "worm" of a beetle is the larva which hatches from its egg. Sometimes it has no eyes, but that does not stop it from eating. It is always very greedy. A beetle larva will eat almost anything but stone or metal. It harms wood, trees, fruit, flowers, grain, furs, and clothes by gnawing and eating these things. The larva of a beetle looks like the larva of a butterfly. It has no wings; in fact, no larva ever has wings. It is interesting to know that **larva** means "mask."

The change of getting wings comes when the larva has gone into its pupa case, or cocoon. Often in this stage, it lies still as if it is asleep or dead. In the pupa stage, it rests in its cocoon, which is shaped like a hen's egg. There the pupa lies in its "cradle," with its legs folded over the front of its body, its wings packed by its side, and its jaws and feelers laid on its chest. It looks very much like a baby asleep in his cradle. It is not pretty like a human baby; in fact, it is ugly to behold. The larva could eat, walk, roll, or swim; but in

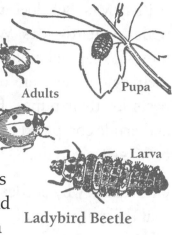

Ladybird Beetle

this little case, the pupa can only wait until it breaks out as an adult beetle. Do you remember what **pupa** means? It means "baby" or "doll."

Finally, the beetle gnaws away at its case and comes out as a full-grown beetle that can fly, swim, eat, and walk. It is often a thing of great beauty. In some books you may read about this insect being in the "image stage." This name is given to the whole, full-grown insect. It means that it has reached the same form that its mother had when she first laid her eggs.

How To Learn About Beetles

No class of insects has been more studied and written about than beetles. Why is this? They are not as wise as the ants. They do not build homes and cities, as bees and wasps do. They do not make honey or wax as busy Mrs. Bee does, and they do not have as many trades as hardy Mrs. Wasp. There are a few beetles, though, that make little mud cells or balls of dirt for their eggs. There are a few others that weave little nests for their pupae. Even so, their work is sloppy and crude compared to the fine work that Mrs. Wasp or Mrs. Bee can do.

One reason why beetles have had so much attention is that there are so many of them and so many different kinds. Another reason is that they live around us so we can observe them. Since their bodies are firm and strong, they can be taken apart so we can study them. Since they do not spoil as fast as soft-bodied insects, the beetles' body parts can be kept a long time after they are dead. The main reason beetles have had so much attention is that their bodies have such beautiful colors and shapes. Often their wing cases, or elytra, are lined and dotted as if carved with great care.

Would you like to have some beetles to keep, to look at and show to your friends? Let me tell you how to catch them. If you dig about the roots of plants or under stones, you will find larvae, pupae, and adult beetles to look at. It is well to seek out these things for yourselves. Handle them gently; these are living things. When you go outside, carry a bottle with a

wide mouth and a good cork. If this
bottle has broken **laurel leaves**[1] in
it, the beetles will die as soon as
you put them in. If you have a little
ether,[2] it will also kill the beetles.
The easiest way is to place the
beetles in a plastic bag or container
and put them into the freezer for
about thirty minutes.

Why do these things kill a beetle
so quickly? Here is a great fact that
you must learn. An insect does not
breathe through its mouth or nose, as you do. It has
no lungs. It breathes through pipes, or tubes, wound
all over its body. These tubes are even found on the
legs and feet of the insect. They are very fine and too
tiny to be seen with the naked eye. These tubes are
held open by a small, stiff,
spiral thread. They reach
the open air through many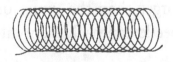
openings, or breathing holes. Now, when you place
the beetle into a bottle with ether or laurel leaves, all

---

1. Dark, glossy leaves from small evergreen trees. Sometimes they are
   called bay, or sweet bay, leaves.

2. Ether is a colorless liquid that burns easily and evaporates quickly.
   This chemical ($C_4H_{10}O$) should be used with parental supervision.

its tubes get filled, and it dies at once. In the freezer, the tubes close up, then the beetle dies.

After your beetle is dead, set it on a piece of cardboard or **balsawood**[3]; you will fasten your beetle on this "spreading board" for safekeeping. Draw the legs, feelers, and jaws into place with a pin or toothpick. Then fasten the beetle to the board with a tiny drop of thick glue placed under its body. You could also put a fine needle or pin through its body and attach it to the board; but be very sure that your beetle is dead first. If you collect beetles in this way, you will soon have many that come in all colors, shapes, and sizes. They may be brown, black, red, green, or golden. It is hard to describe how beautiful these beetles truly are! Put some on the cardboard or balsawood with their wing cases raised up and their flying wings drawn out from underneath—the underwings being larger than the upper ones. It is a wonder that the beetle can pack them into such small cases.

The feelers, or antennae, of beetles take many forms. Some are like plumes, others are like scales or leaves, and still others like clubs. Some antennae are nearly round like balls, others are cone-shaped, and still

---

3. A light, sturdy wood that can be purchased at most hobby shops or home centers. These *spreading boards* are used for mounting insects.

others are plain and straight. Some are even bent like a new moon.

A farmer or gardener will like your beetles better dead than alive. As he will tell you, the beetles and their larvae are very greedy things. They often eat leaves and spoil crops and trees.

The Rose Beetle

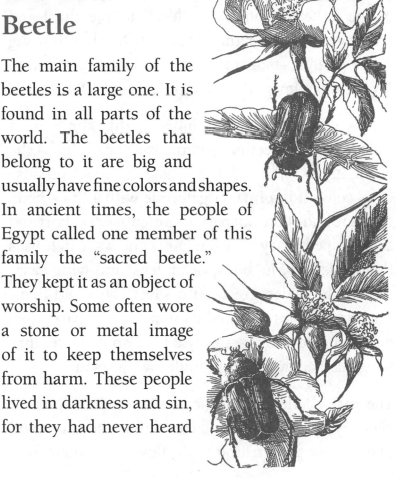

The main family of the beetles is a large one. It is found in all parts of the world. The beetles that belong to it are big and usually have fine colors and shapes. In ancient times, the people of Egypt called one member of this family the "sacred beetle." They kept it as an object of worship. Some often wore a stone or metal image of it to keep themselves from harm. These people lived in darkness and sin, for they had never heard of the great Creator God who only should be worshiped.

The Second Commandment says, "You shall not make for yourself any carved image, or any likeness of anything that is in heaven above, or that is in the earth beneath, or that is in the water under the earth; you shall not bow down to them nor serve them. For I, the Lord your God, am a jealous God, visiting the iniquity of the fathers upon the children to the third and fourth generations of those who hate Me, but showing mercy to thousands, to those who love Me and keep My commandments" (Deuteronomy 5:8–10).

Let us now study one member of this family. It is called the **rose beetle**. Its name is as beautiful as the beetle itself. Some call it the "golden beetle" because of its color. It is a fine, large beetle with a thick body that is round at the tail part. Its antennae are short and club-shaped. They have ten joints and wave lightly as the beetle flies. Its body, head, legs, and wing cases are a rich, golden green with silver spots and lines. This beetle does not hold its wing cases apart when it flies. It tips the cases only a little so its wide, thin wings can come out from underneath them.

The rose beetle is seen mostly in May and June. It chooses a pretty home and eats dainty food. You will find it in the garden around the flowers. Its main food is nectar and flower petals. Its mouth is not tough but soft and skinlike. The rose beetle chooses the brightest and largest flowers for its home and food. It digs deep into the hearts of the roses. It sucks the nectar and chews the petals. It also likes the sunshine, and when it flashes about in the light, it looks like a piece of melted gold with green tints on it.

When the mother rose beetle wishes to lay her eggs, she finds a place at the foot of a tree. She goes down in the ground among the roots, where the wood is old and soft. Then she puts her eggs between the bark and the wood. Sometimes she changes her whole plan and puts her eggs into an ant's nest! The ants do not seem to mind at all.

The larvae of the rose beetle are fat, round things that look like thick, white worms. Their heads are round and pale brown in color. Their thin skin has hairs on it. The larvae move very slowly and always rest on one side. They have strong jaws, and their antennae have five joints. A number of these larvae live together. They are dull and lazy and always eating. They eat leaves and soft wood. While the weather is warm, the larvae keep near the top of the soil. When it is cold, they dig down, even one or two feet, and lie asleep until spring comes again. They live in this way for three years.

Then the larvae make round or egg-shaped balls with bits of earth, bits of dead leaves, and grass. They may even use the wood or sawdust they have cut up with their jaws. They fasten all these things together with "glue" from their mouths. When the larvae are shut up in these balls, they change very quickly. At first, the cases, or cocoons, seem full of a milky fluid. Then their legs and wings grow. After a few weeks the white larvae have changed into fine beetles that look like jewels. Some of these beetles are so fine that they are put into hoops of gold for earrings and broaches. On the island of Luzon in the Philippines, ladies keep rose beetles in tiny cages for pets!

There is another beetle much like the rose beetle. It is called the **June bug**, and it is golden brown in color. These beetles come in great numbers, eating the leaves of trees and even killing the trees themselves in this way. Since each mother lays about forty eggs, it is no wonder there are so many of them. After the larvae hatch, they also do a lot of damage; the only difference is that they destroy plants by eating the roots.

Since June bugs do not like the sun, they hide all day in the shade; but at night, they like to fly. They especially like to get into a room where a light is shining brightly. June bugs blunder about making a great buzzing noise with their hornlike wings. They even hit their heads on walls and panes of glass. Some people are afraid of them, but that is foolish because June bugs cannot harm them in any way.

If you watch these beetles, see how they lift their wing-covers when they are about to fly. Look well at the folding of the inner wings. If you open a door or window on a warm night and set a light in the room, you may soon catch many beautiful beetles which like to fly about feasting on sweet, white flowers that open after dark.

Giants and Princes

Beetles vary much in size. Some are so small that you can hardly see them as they creep along in the grass. Others are so large that a child might fear them. He

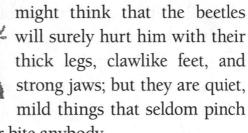

might think that the beetles will surely hurt him with their thick legs, clawlike feet, and strong jaws; but they are quiet, mild things that seldom pinch or bite anybody.

Why do these beetles have such tough coats that look like armor? These "coats of armor" keep them from harm. Nevertheless, fish, birds, and other animals like to eat them and their grubs. Many more animals might eat these beetles if they did not have their hornlike coats to shield them. Enough are killed and eaten, though, to prevent the world from being overrun with them. Beetles have very few weapons, so they live under stones and among roots. They also like to dig about in the earth to hide. Their main protection, however, is their hornlike bodies.

The **stag beetle** is a kind of beetle that protects itself with its strong jaws. When it is attacked, it gives its enemies a good pinch. It is called a stag beetle because the male stag beetle has large jaws, or **mandibles**, that look like the antlers of a stag, or male deer.

Stag Beetle

The **oil beetle** is another kind of beetle that protects itself with an oil that it drops from its legs when it is touched. This oil has a bad smell and can make a blister on the skin. Because of this oil, people let them alone, and perhaps small animals do the same.

There is another kind of beetle that carries a "gun"! This is like a weapon with several barrels; it can be fired three or four times without being reloaded! "Oh, how can that be?" you might ask. Near the tail of the "gun beetle" is a little sac, or bag, full of fluid. When an enemy comes near him, Mr. Gun Beetle throws off a tiny drop of this fluid as he runs. The fluid flies out of the sac with a little bang. It sounds like the blast of a tiny gun and gives off a kind of mist, or blue smoke. Three or four of these shots follow each other. Big beetles like to chase this small fellow, but when Mr. Gun Beetle's tiny gun goes off in the face of his enemy, the big beetle backs away. Then it folds down its

Gun Beetle

antennae and stands still. It acts very much like a dog when it drops its tail between its legs and runs off! This little gun-toting beetle likes to live in damp places. Often a group of them will hide under a stone. If you lift up the stone, these poor beetles get in such a panic that they begin to fire off their guns like a squad of soldiers.

Since I have talked some about little beetles, let me now tell you about a few large ones. The very large beetles live in hot lands and are **scarce**. Some have jaws that are large and curved like a crab's claw. At first sight, you might think they are crabs. The colors of these big beetles are often quite splendid. Some of them have long horns on the front of their heads.

Others have very large back legs with such strange shapes; in fact, they do not even look like beetles.

One large beetle is so big that it is called a "giant." Another is called the **Goliath beetle**; it is named after the huge man whom King David slew. You can read about David and Goliath in 1 Samuel 17. Others are named after Atlas and Hercules who are giants from tales told from ancient times. There is still

Goliath Beetle

another great beetle in Brazil called the "prince of beetles." It gets this name from its size and beauty. Some of these "princes" have been sold for two hundred dollars each.

Some of these giant beetles have large knobs, or "teeth," upon their jaws; they use them to crush and break their food. These "teeth" are like the knobs on Mr. Crab's claw which he uses for playing a tune. Mr. Beetle can also use his knobs to make music, and he is fond of his own tunes. Often he makes a shrill humming or buzzing sound for hours by rubbing his wing cases, or elytra, with his "teeth."

When you walk in the field, you might carry a bottle with a wide mouth. In this you can collect beetles to study. It may be very pleasant to study them when you go home, but be sure to have something in the bottle to kill them first. If you do not, they become frightened and are likely to pull each other to pieces when they are shut up in such a small space.

Burying Beetles

Once, when I was young, I saw a dark beetle standing on its back legs. It was holding its fore legs clasped over its head, as you would hold your hands in prayer. An old man who was nearby said, "That is a holy bug, and it shows what man ought to do. It is saying its prayers. People call it the 'praying beetle.'" I think the old man meant what he said; but, of course, the beetle was neither holy nor praying. Its strange way of standing is only one of the remarkable habits that beetles enjoy.

Now I will tell you of a curious habit of the **dung beetle**. Very often on the road you will see Mrs. Beetle rolling about a small ball the size of a marble. The ball is made of dirt, or some soft matter, and is often larger than the beetle herself. Nevertheless, she rolls it with ease, for she is very strong. Mrs. Dung Beetle is not playing marbles or baseball, though; she is only doing her work.

First of all, Mrs. Dung Beetle flies about looking for a good place to lay her eggs. Then she lays them in a morsel of dirt or dung. Finally, she goes to work with all her might making her ball. Mrs. Dung Beetle molds the soft matter over her eggs. As she rolls it about, it grows larger, as your snowball grows when you roll it about in the snow. When the larvae hatch from their eggs, this ball will be their food until they are strong enough to crawl about and seek food for themselves.

When the ball is done, Mrs. Dung Beetle does not leave it in the road for wheels to run over it or feet to trample it. She looks for a place where the larvae will be safe and feed well when they hatch from their eggs. She either drags the ball along between her back feet, pushes it with her front or back feet, or rolls it along toward the safe place which she has wisely chosen. If the ground is so rough that Mrs. Dung Beetle cannot move her ball on the ground, she carries it on her head. Her flat head has some tiny knobs which helps her hold the load firmly in place as she carries it along. Did you ever see a boy carry a box, pail, or bundle on his head? Mrs. Dung Beetle does the same thing.

Perhaps Mrs. Dung Beetle finds that she cannot take her ball to a safe place without help, so she flies off to get help. Soon she comes back with other beetles of her own kind. Then she tells them what she needs, and they all help her until her ball is where she wishes it to be. I have seen four or five beetles at work on one ball. When the ball is in the right spot, Mrs. Dung Beetle digs a hole with her jaws and hornlike front legs. Then she rolls the ball into it. She fills up the hole with earth and presses it down flat.

This is not the only beetle that buries its eggs. There is another one called the **sexton beetle**, or carrion beetle. When it finds a dead bird, mouse, frog, or other small animal, it begins to bury it by digging a little grave for it. This is why it is called a **sexton**. A sexton was a caretaker of a church and its adjacent graveyard; he had the job of burying the dead. This beetle begins to dig under the dead body. As it takes out the earth, the dead creature sinks more and more. At last it is deep enough to be covered, as a coffin is covered in a grave. In this way the sexton beetle helps to keep the earth and air clean. Is that why it buries things? Oh, no! The beetle does this to make a good place for its eggs.

Sexton beetles may be black, orange, red or yellow. They are rather large and live in pairs. You might think that the sexton and dung beetles would be dirty from their work, but they are not. These beetles have a kind of oil all over their bodies which keeps dirt from sticking to them. This oil always keeps them clean and bright. Burying beetles also have a keen

sense of smell. They can smell a dead animal even if it is a long way off.

Let us watch Mr. and Mrs. Sexton Beetle at work. Here is a dead mouse. These two beetles come flying through the air with their wings humming. When they land, Mr. Sexton Beetle goes briskly to his work, and Mrs. Sexton Beetle stands looking on. Her work in this world is not to dig but to lay eggs. Before the work begins, they both make a good meal off the dead mouse. All sexton beetles eat flesh. Mr. Sexton Beetle works a while, then he drops down, as if very tired, and sleeps. Then up he gets and plows furrow after furrow about the mouse. He uses his head for a plow. Now the dead body has sunk out of sight. Mr. Sexton Beetle has covered it with the earth he took out from the grave which he made. He makes all the little grave smooth and trim.

What is this strange little fellow doing now? He is making a little side door into the grave. Now he and Mrs. Beetle are walking in to take another meal from the mouse. When their dinner is over, Mrs. Beetle lays some eggs in the dead body. She knows that when the larvae hatch from the eggs, they will like to eat the food which they will find all around them. The larvae of the sexton beetle looks much like a beach flea, or "sand hopper." After the eggs are laid,

Mr. and Mrs. Beetle come out into the air. Then Mr. Beetle fills up the doorway, and off the two fly to find other things to bury.

Does the strength of beetles surprise you? They have strong, sharp jaws. Once I found a fine grass-green beetle with silver spots. I wanted him for my collection of beetles. I tied him up in a piece of cloth to carry him home. The cloth was doubled over, but he ate a hole right through it; then away he went. Another time, I shut up ten beetles in a box. I forgot them for two days. When I opened the box, they were all dead. They had killed each other. The box had in it only heads, legs, and wings. The last beetle that had been left had lost his legs and wings. He had won the battle but died on the field.

The Story of the Stag Beetle

Stag beetles are among the largest beetles that are found in North America. They get this name from the size of their jaws. If you look at the picture, you will see that the great jaws look like antlers. If you should ever see the head of a stag, or male deer, you may notice that this beetle's jaws are much like the stag's antlers in shape. These jaws can give a very hard pinch in time of need. This is why some people call it the "pinching beetle." Still, you do not need to be afraid of the stag beetle; he will not hurt you.

If you look closely, you will see that Mr. Stag Beetle's great jaws have knobs on the inner edge. He is the only beetle that has these knobs, or "horns." Mrs.

Stag Beetle has small jaws, and her head is not as wide as her shoulders. Mr. Stag Beetle, however, has a very wide head which he needs to hold up his big jaws.

If you examine a beetle, you will see that its feelers, or antennae, are like plumes of feathers. These "feathers" are set so that the beetle can fold them on each other into a clublike bundle, as you would fold a fan. They are called "scale feelers." Mr. Stag Beetle has curious feelers as well. They are also made in scales, but he cannot close them into a bundle. The scales are set like the teeth of a comb. Perhaps his "comb feelers" help him in cleaning his body and legs. During the day, Mr. Stag Beetle crawls about on the trees; then he flies around by night.

Mrs. Stag Beetle usually lays her eggs in the trunk of an old oak or willow tree. When her baby larvae hatch, they begin to eat the bark, wood, leaves, and roots of the old tree. They have six strong legs and a pair of strong jaws for cutting the leaves and wood. These larvae are very large, and they lie with their bodies curled in a half circle. If you look closely at the larva, you will see nine round spots along the sides of its body on the middle rings, or segments. The larva looks as if it is wearing a coat with big buttons on the side. The amazing thing is that these "buttons" are the air holes through which this larva breathes.

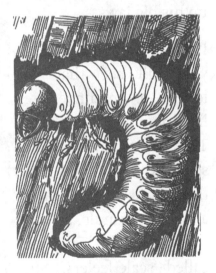

Now let us review how an insect breathes. You know that when you draw the air in through your nose and mouth, air fills your lungs so you can breathe. You also know that the insect breathes through long, fine tubes. They are kept open with a stiff, spiral thread which winds all over its body. These tubes have openings for air to pass in and out, and they can open and close. In shape, they are a little like the lip of a glass jar. These are the openings that we see so clearly along the side of the body of this stag beetle larva. Both the larva and the pupa must breathe, or they cannot live.

The larva of a stag beetle lives and grows for four years or more, then it passes into the pupa stage. When it is ready to change, it makes a case, or cocoon, for itself with the fine chips from which it has been sucking juice. It binds this sort of coarse sawdust together with "glue" from its mouth. When the stag beetle finally comes out of its cocoon, it is a fine looking beetle. Its head and chest are black with tiny dots like carvings, and its elytra, or wing cases, are a deep, reddish-brown.

There are some kinds of stag beetles that never get large, strong "antlers." We do not know why this happens; but we do know that Mr. Stag Beetle who has antlers fights with and beats his cousins who have none. They are fond of fighting; in this way, they are like Mr. Crab. Stag beetles enjoy dueling with each other, but Mrs. Stag Beetle does not behave in this way. She looks on at the fight, but takes no part in it.

Her business is to lay eggs in safe places. She has no time to fight; but then, she has no "antlers"!

Mr. Beetle with the Short Coat

I shall now tell you about a very interesting kind of beetle. If you ever find one member of this family, you will say, "This poor beetle has outgrown his coat!" You will say that when you see how very short his elytra, or wing cases, are. But no! The beetle has not outgrown his "coat." Insects do not grow after they leave the pupa case. Mr. Beetle and his "coat" are both of the same size as when he came out of his cocoon. It is the fashion in his family to wear short clothes! The flying wings of this beetle are large, but the elytra are very short. They do not cover half the length of its body. Yet this beetle can fold up and tuck his flying wings under these short wing cases.

Most of the short-coat beetles are small. The largest ones only grow up to an inch long. They are very lively insects and very greedy, too. Some of these beetles eat only animal food, for which they are always busy hunting. Others are fond of mushrooms.

Some "short-coats" have a bad smell. No doubt they have this bad smell to keep away creatures that would eat them. People also do not care to touch them. In this way, the smell keeps these beetles from harm. It would be easy to hurt them since their hard shell coat is so short. However, all "short-coats" do not have a bad smell; while some beetles with "long coats" do have this foul odor. Yet there are also beetles that smell like roses or like musk.

Some of the "short-coat" beetles curl the back part of their body over and hold it up above their backs. If they had long, hard coats, they could not do that. One very large "short-coat" beetle is called the "coach horse." The larvac of this beetle look like the full-grown insect. They carry their tails overhead, in the same way. These larvae can run fast and seek food all day long. They often hide under stones; and in the winter, they go down deeper underground. They are fierce, and they eat animal flesh. The pupae live only about three weeks in their cocoons. Their shiny, gold pupa cases have an odd shape, like a wedge with a rounded top, and a plume of hairs in front.

In Brazil people can find one kind of the "short-coat" beetle living in the nests of termites, or white ants. Beetles that live with termites are very strange creatures. The back parts of their bodies are too large compared to the front parts. They look like great balls that are turned up over the upper parts of their backs. These are the only beetles that do not lay eggs and go off and leave them. They keep their eggs in this large, round part of their bodies until they hatch. Then the little larvae come out alive. Why do the termites allow these beetles to live with them? Perhaps it is because they do not make any trouble, so the termites do not care one way or the other. On the other hand, these beetles may have a way of making honeydew, like the little aphids do for the honey ants; if so, they pay for their house rent with it!

There are other "short-coat" beetles which do not have these big, round bodies. They lay their eggs like other beetles, yet they live in anthills. Perhaps these beetles and their larvae like to feed on the husks and rubbish they may find in the anthill. 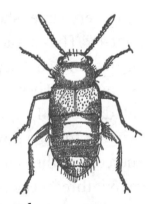 Nevertheless, the ants do not drive them out.

The "short-coat" beetles are not the only ones that take up lodging in another's home. Perhaps you have heard your mother say, "The moths have gotten into my furs!" If she looks at the furs, she may find, not only moths, but also small beetles. They have a wonderful time eating up the fur! Such beetles destroy furs, skins, skin rugs, and animals that have been preserved and stuffed. Their greedy larvae also can make much **havoc**. These larvae are like tiny black worms. They are fond of ham, bacon, and lard.

The Little Watermen

You may have read about spiders that live on land and run on the water. Likewise, there are land beetles and **water beetles**. The water spiders have rafts, boats, skates, and diving bells. They sit and float on lily leaves. Their homes are cool and bright under the clear, still waters. There is also a happy race of beetles that have all the same things. The story of these beetles is like the tale of a fairy prince, yet it is true.

God created all living things to live in their own, special place. The animals that live in cold lands have thick fur. Birds are made with light bodies and feathered wings so they can fly easily. The fish have scaly, pointed, slippery bodies, so they can glide swiftly through the water. Therefore, you must expect to find that the water beetles are not quite like the land beetles. They have bodies created to live in their water home. If you place a water beetle beside a land beetle, you will see that the parts of the water beetle fit more closely together than the land beetle's. They join each other to form a smooth, watertight case. When we build a boat, is it not our first concern to make it airtight so it will not leak? So it is with God when He created the water beetles.

Since Mr. Water Beetle will swim much and walk very little, his first and second pairs of legs are small and feeble. His back legs, however, are wide and strong and reach far back. They are used for swimming. Mr. Swimming Crab also has broad back legs which he uses for oars or paddles. Mr. Water Beetle's legs are made in much the same way, but his legs have hairs, or **bristles**, upon them. In addition, he has flat pads on his feet, like water spiders do. The hairs on these pads hold tiny bubbles of air which helps him to float.

Though Mr. Water Beetle was created to walk a little, he was fitted with fine, large wings to fly a lot. In fact, he enjoys flying. When he wishes to fly, he does not rise straight out of the water. First he climbs up the stem of some plant. Then, when he is high enough to make a good start, he spreads his lovely wings and skims away. Very often Mr. Water Beetle flies at night and seems to delight in the clear moonlight. The water of his pond spreads out like a sheet of silver, and the crickets chirp in the grass. The air is moist and cool; it is sweet with the scent of flowers. On such nights, Mr. Water Beetle rises quite high into the air and flies here and there, as if full of joy. Then he turns, closes his wings, and drops into the water with a splash, like a stone.

The larvae of water beetles live in the water as their parents

Larva of a Water Beetle

do. They are very greedy and hunt for their food as if they were angry. They have large jaws, shaped like a **sickle**. Their bodies are long and narrow, and they have six tiny eyes on each side of their heads. With so many eyes, the larvae can see all about them, which helps them keep out of danger. They also see bugs which they wish to catch. Their straight, narrow bodies dart through the water with such quick motion. Then the larvae pounce on their prey, and their curved jaws hold it fast.

If you watch the ponds, you may see a water beetle floating with its head down, and the tip of its tail stuck out of the water. What does it mean by that strange action? It is getting air to breathe. Though it lives under the water, it breathes air, and it is filling up its "diving bell"; or, rather, it is turning itself into a "diving bell." How does it do that? Let us see. This beetle's elytra, or wing cases, are airtight. The openings of its breathing tubes open under the wing covers. When it has used all the fresh air it had, it wants some more. So it comes to the top of the water, turns its head down, and spreads out its feet to balance itself. Then, with a little jerk, it drives out any air that is yet under its elytra. Then it draws in fresh air, shuts its elytra up close, and goes down with plenty of fresh, pure air to breathe.

Did you ever see a **whirligig beetle** with its fine bronze color? It takes its name from the top, or whirligig, because it spins round and round and round. Go to the pond, and you will see one of these merry creatures. It acts as if it is so happy that it cannot keep still. The whirligig uses its back legs for oars, and its front legs for rudders. It also has eyes that are divided; each eye seems to have a pair of eyes on each side of its

head. One half the eye looks up, and the other half looks down. These small beetles whirl, whirl, whirl; then they stand still for a second. If you make a dart at them, and try to catch them, you will find that it is not easy to do so. These "whirlers" lay their eggs on leaves above water. Their larvae spin silk pupa cases which hang on leaves or stems above the top of the water. These and other water beetles live in ponds or very quiet streams, not in swift water.

Uses of Beetles

Of what use are beetles? Wise people have not yet found out everything about the use of beetles. Yet you have learned that some of them **devour** or bury dead animals that would be bad if they were left lying about on the ground. These beetles help to keep the world clean. In addition, other beetles eat insects that harm plants. Still others make good food for fish, birds, and other creatures. Nevertheless, many of the beetles do much harm to plants, clothes, and other valuable things. On the whole, it seems that beetles are more beautiful than useful!

Among all the creatures you study, you will find points of likeness between one creature and another. So it is with the beetle. For example, a fly has a little pair of false wings, called alulae; they are found at the base of its true wings. One of the beetles also has similar pair of "winglets," or alulae. In other words, the beetle may be like a fly in one way, like a spider in another way, and like a crab in still another way. Comparing the likenesses—and differences—of God's creatures is a wonderful way to learn more about His wonderful works.

I hope this brief look at beetles and their way of life will make you wish to study them more. Studying about these fascinating creatures in books is rewarding, but going outdoors and discovering their ways for yourself is even better.

Review

1. Insects are divided into what two classes? To what class of insects does a ladybird belong?

2. With what is a beetle's body covered? In what way is a beetle like a crab?

3. Describe a beetle's wing covers. Where are its flying wings located?   What does it do with its wing covers when it flies?

4. Describe a beetle. What colors does a beetle have?

5. Which is the largest family of insects? Why have people studied beetles so much?

6. What changes does the beetle make before it is full-grown?

7. Where are the eggs of beetles laid? How much time do some beetles spend as eggs, larvae, and pupae?

8. Describe a beetle larva. How does this larva behave? Where is a beetle larva likely to be found? What does larva mean?

9. How is the pupa packed in the pupa case? Where is a beetle pupa likely to be found? What does pupa mean?

10. Describe how an insect breathes.

11. How do beetles injure plants?

12. Describe a rose beetle.

13. What can you tell me about giant beetles? In what country does the prince of beetles live?

14. How do beetles make a noise or tune?

15. How does the dung beetle make a place for her eggs? Of what use are these beetles?

16. Describe how the sexton beetle buries a mouse or bird. Why does it do this?

17. Describe a stag beetle. Do all stag beetles have horns?

18. Tell me about the "short-coat" beetles.

Chapter Four
All About Barnacles

What a Fisherman Told

One day on the beach, I saw a man mending a net. He took from the net two, small, shell-like things that clung to the meshes of the net. They were white and hard. They looked like two or three shells, one put inside the other.

The fisherman said, "There are in the world more of these things than there are leaves on the trees, I think."

"Where do they grow, Mr. Fisherman?"

"It is easier," said the fisherman, "to say where they do not grow, unless I just say, they grow wherever there is seawater. The pier yonder, below the **high-water mark**,[1] is covered with hundreds of them. All the rocks that we see bare at low tide are white with them. Every log or stick that drifts on the sea has them on it. All the old shells on the beach, and many new shells, have dozens fastened on them.

---

1. A mark showing the highest level that a body of water has risen. It is caused by the flow of tides or flooding.

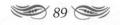

"I have seen an old king crab crawl up the beach," the fisherman said. "He had his shell so coated with these things, that it seemed as if he had two shells; one on top of the other. His load was so heavy that he could hardly walk.

"I have also seen them growing in the skins of whales, sharks, and other fish. I have sailed all around the world, and I have found these things everywhere."

"What do you call them, Mr. Fisherman?"

"Some call them 'sea acorns,' some 'sea rosebuds.' These are pretty names; but **barnacle** is the right name."

"Do you know, Mr. Fisherman, that they are cousins of the crabs? They are a kind of shellfish."

"I'll never believe *that*," said the fisherman. "They do not *look* like crabs. When I was a boy, folks told me

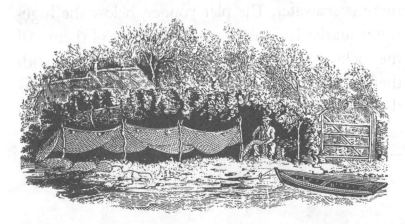

that out of these shells came little birds that grew into geese. I saw a picture once, of a tree all covered with big barnacles, and out of each one hung a little bird's head. Is that tale true? They were not quite like these barnacles!"

"No, Mr. Fisherman, it is not at all true. Birds never grow from barnacles. That is a silly, old fable."

"Well," said the fisherman, "once in the water, I saw something hanging out of the shell of a fellow like this. It opened and shut, and it looked a little like a bird's foot."

"It was a foot, Mr. Fisherman, but not a bird's foot. It was Mr. Barnacle's own foot, and since he has no hands, he uses his feet to catch his dinner."

"I know," said the fisherman, "that horsehairs in ponds will turn into long worms; but I never did think these shells would turn into birds."

"With all due respect, Mr. Fisherman, horsehairs will never turn into worms. Yet long, thin, black worms in ponds look so much like the hairs of a horse's tail, that some people think they must have come from its tail; but it is not so. Horsehairs will always be horsehairs, and all worms hatch from eggs which were laid to bring out worms."

"It is a pity," said the fisherman, "that when I was a boy in school my books did not tell me of these things. It would have been nice to know what I was looking at as I went about the world."

Now let us study these barnacles of which our fisherman spoke. He was right when he told us about their number and where they grow. He told us what he knew, and that was based on what he had seen. There are two kinds of barnacles—those that have "stalks," and those that have no stalks. The kind that has no stalks is the kind you will see more often, though there are plenty of the other kind. The stalkless, or "acorn," barnacles fasten themselves flat upon whatever they grow. If you try to pull one off a stone, you will not be able to do it while the barnacle is alive. If it is dead or dying, though, you may be able to remove it. After these barnacles have been dead for some time, they drop from their places and leave room for others to grow.

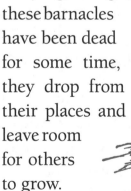

Stalkless Barnacle   **Stalk Barnacle**

All barnacles do not fix themselves upon non-living things, such as stones, wood, or shells. Many of them fasten upon living creatures that carry them about from place to place. Perhaps they enjoy travel! Many sharks have barnacles growing on them. The stalk of the barnacle has little hollow hairs, which enter into the flesh of the shark and hold fast there. Others have been found keeping house upon the whale's skin, and yet others on the shells of turtles. The barnacles which you find by the shore are small things; you can hold several of them in your hand at once. In some parts of the world, there is a large kind of barnacles that people eat like we eat oysters or mussels. There are other huge barnacles that live deep down in the ocean; they are so big that some of you would hardly be able to lift one.

The Barnacle Family

Mr. Barnacle has been given a Latin name, **Cirripede**, which means "curled-foot." People thought his little fine curled up feet looked like small curls of hair. His body is like a small bag, or sac, with the six pairs of little curly feet placed at one end. His body is made of rings like the body of an insect. All six pairs of legs are on the chest rings. Each leg has two joints and a little branch like a fine **fringe**. The hard shell-like cover of the barnacle is made of plates that lie closely together—one upon another. When they are closed, they look something like buds on trees, or young pine cones. When the fringes of Mr. Barnacle's feet wave out between the edges of the shell-like plates, it looks as if the buds were about to open into a flower.

Mr. Barnacle is more like his far-off cousin Mr. Crab when he is little than when he is an adult. He must be firmly fastened upon some other creature or thing. Mr. Barnacle's family is divided into two classes, according to the way in which they fasten themselves upon objects—stalk barnacles and stalkless barnacles. A stalk barnacle has plates which form a three-cornered shell. It grows firmly upon some object by a small, soft stalk that can bend about easily. A stalkless barnacle has a shell shaped like an acorn, or like a rosebud with the top bitten off. Instead of a stalk, it is held fast to an object on which it grows by a thin plate of shell at its broad, or flat end. This plate has a tiny hole in the center.

When you first see Mr. Barnacle, you probably would not think he is a relative of Mr. Crab. When he is fully grown, he does not look at all like the Crab family. When crabs and barnacles are very young, though, they look more like each other.

Let us look at Mr. Acorn Barnacle. He has a shell-like "coat" that is made in plates, which look as if two or three shells were set one over another. These plates grow when bits of lime are added, as Mr. Conch adds to his shell. Mr. Acorn Barnacle's hard, white coat is lined with a very thin skin which holds his coat together. This skin often has a faint, pretty tint. When he sheds his skin, like Mr. Crab does, his "coat" has room to grow.

A stalk barnacle has a long, fleshlike stalk which moves and sways with the motion of the water. It looks much like a little, strange, pale plum hung by a thick stalk. The head of the stalk barnacle is the end which clings to a stone, log, shell, or fish. Mr. Barnacle has two feelers that turn into two fine tubes, or pipes. His feelers have little glands, or sacs, which make a very strong cement. This cement is like glue but is much stronger and stiffer. Mr. Barnacle uses this cement to

fasten himself to his place. After he has settled down in life, he never wanders about any more.

Did Mr. Barnacle ever go abroad? Oh, yes! When he was young, he swam about in the water in a very brisk way. Let us hear about that. Mr. Barnacle makes the same changes of life that an insect does. First he is an egg, then a larva, then a pupa, and at last a steady old barnacle. The only difference is that the barnacle larva makes two or three changes of shape before it turns into a pupa. Mr. Barnacle grows fast and changes his coat often when he is young.

Here is Mrs. Acorn Barnacle fastened on a stone. She is about as big as the end of your little finger. She has some eggs which she packs into the shape of a small leaf. She tucks this leaf of eggs into a fold of the thin skin that lines her thick shell. As the eggs get ready to hatch into larvae, Mrs. Acorn Barnacle is also growing and making more shell. When she is ready to enlarge her outer shell, the inside skin cracks apart and falls off. By degrees, she becomes quite large as fresh shell grows from within. When her old

inside skin falls off, the eggs are set free. Out of them come the larvae. The larvae are active, hungry little fellows, who know how to swim as soon as they are loose in the water. God is wise because of the way He created these larvae to live on their own.

The larva acts as if it likes to be free from the shell prison. It darts about in the sea, and each day its shape changes. It has one eye, a mouth, two feelers like horns, and six legs. It can swim and walk over seaweed. Some parts of this lively, little larva will one day turn into tubes to make cement to hold it fast to a stone. Then it will be a stay-at-home barnacle all the rest of its life. When the larva becomes a pupa, it drifts about until at last it is time for it to stop traveling and keep still. Then it fixes itself by its head to the place that will always be its home. After that, all it has to do is to fish and eat. As it makes new shell, it will enlarge the old shell.

By and by, Mr. Barnacle has a hard shell of many plates, and his eye has gone down near his stomach. Do you think that helps him to see what he eats now? The rest of his head has gone off with his feelers to make cement and shell. His odd legs are not used for walking but for fishing; and his mouth is near his feet!

A Fishing Party

Did you ever go fishing? Did you fish with a rod and line? Or, did you sit on a pier and let your line drop into the water from your hand? Or, did you go out with the boats and see the men throw a net into the water? There are many ways of fishing, and now I shall tell you of some strange little fishers and their ways. Why did you want to catch fish? Oh, just for fun! My little fishers fish for food, and they eat their "fish" without cooking them. Their "fish" are so small that you cannot see them without the help of a magnifying glass.

I saw a fishing party today. There were twenty fishers all dressed in white coats, and they all sat on one rock. "What a big rock!" you may blurt out. You had better say, "Oh, what little fishers!" For, to tell you the truth, I covered the whole party up with one of my hands! Was this a fairy fishing party? No; it was a barnacle fishing party. I will tell you about it.

The sun shone on the water, the sea was still, and the tide was slowly going out. At half low tide, a gray rock lay in the water. The water was yet about two or three inches above the top of the rock. On this rock were about twenty, stalkless acorn barnacles—clean and white. They were of the size of small acorns. You must know that barnacles grow and come in many sizes. Some are the size of a small button. Others are of the size of a small acorn, or of the end of your little finger.

As I looked at these twenty little fishers, the plates of the shells were opened a little. Out of the top of each shell came a fine little plume, like five or six tiny feathers. This plume waved up and down in the

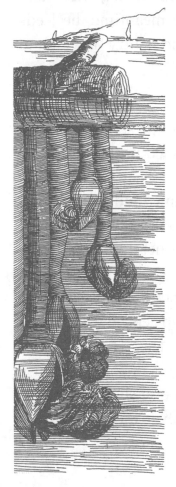

water. It seemed to open and shut gently, as you would open and shut your hand. Every now and then this little plume was drawn completely back into the shell. A minute later, it came out again and waved as before. What did all this mean? It meant that the barnacles were having a fishing party. They were catching their dinner while the tide was over their shells. Mr. Crab gets his dinner at low tide and hides at high tide. Mr. Barnacle fishes and eats at high tide. At low tide he shuts his shell house and clings to his place. He is waiting for the tide to come up and cover him once more.

When Mr. Barnacle opens and shuts this fine plume, it is his net or set of lines with which he fishes for little live creatures from the water. He tangles his prey, or food, up in his fine plumes. Among the things he catches are tiny crabs, too small for the naked eye to see. When the plume net is full, he draws it into his shell. Then he empties it into his mouth. After this, he puts his plume out of his house once more to fish for other things. In the meantime, he feeds on what he has taken. He has no pantry in which to store things, as Mr. Crab has.

Near this fishing party on the rock, drifted a log. On the under side of the log were some stalk barnacles. They were fishing too. They fished in the same way and for the same kind of things. They opened their shells, pushed out a lovely plume, and caught food in their meshes. Do their nets ever break and need to be mended as the fisherman's net does? No doubt, if they do, new pieces will soon grow. Their nets are the barnacles' feet. If any of them are lost or hurt, others will grow, just as Mr. Crab gets new legs when some are gone. Notice these tiny legs. They look very much like a cluster of long fingers or toes. They use them to fish for food. For what else should they use them? Nothing, because they never walk or swim.

A Last Look at Mr. Barnacle

It is well to know all you can about barnacles, for you will see them wherever you go by the seaside. If you study them, do not believe foolish things about them, like Mr. Fisherman who refused to believe the truth. Will it not be pleasant to think of what you know of their story? When you see an acorn barnacle fastened to a stone, you can think of the days when it was young and went sailing about. I wonder if it calls those days "the good old times!" When you see a stalk barnacle swinging in the water, you can think of what a good time it is having, fishing with its pretty feet. The stalkless barnacles also have, from their shape, a name which means "acorn." You will find the Latin names easy to learn when you are older and study more.

The acorn shells can live out of water for a few hours at a time. When the tide is low, many of them are left high and dry. But if they should be out of water too long, they would die for want of food and water. Perhaps, also, the dry heat of the air kills them. If you wish to study them for yourselves, take home a stone, shell, or stick, with some of them on it. Put it in a bowl of seawater. Soon they will open their shells and begin fishing.

Those barnacles which fasten themselves upon living fish, sharks, or whales, bury their heads and tubes in the skins of these animals. I wonder if the whales and sharks feel them and do not like them. The barnacles that make the most trouble are those which fasten themselves upon the outside of ships. The bottoms of ships are often covered with barnacles. They make the hull of the ship rough and heavy. That hinders its motion through the water. In such a case the ship must be put into a dry dock. There it is scraped clean. Because of this trouble and waiting, sailors dislike barnacles. They often say that they wish there were none.

You need not expect to see the young barnacles swimming about in the water. They are very tiny creatures, about the shape of an apple seed. If you should see them, I think you would never guess what they are.

For a great while, people thought barnacles were not worth much study. They called them "shellfish" and did not dream what wonders were hidden in their shell-like plates. At last, when wise men knocked at Mr. Barnacle's house door, and said, "Come out and tell us your secrets," they found he was one of the most interesting little creatures.

Review

1. What did the old fisherman say about the number of barnacles that exist?

2. Do horsehairs ever become worms? What was the silly, old fable about a bird coming from a barnacle?

3. What two kinds of barnacles are there? What does an acorn barnacle look like?

4. During a barnacle's life, when does it sail about? When does it fasten to one place for life? What holds a barnacle firmly to a rock?

5. Describe a stalk barnacle. What does the Latin name of the barnacle family mean?

6. How do barnacles get their food? Describe a barnacle fishing party.

7. What does a barnacle shed as he grows? How do the shell-like plates of a barnacle become larger?

8. Are barnacles ever eaten?

9. How long can barnacles live out of water?

10. What does a barnacle eat? What does a barnacle use for a fishing net?

11. Where is a barnacle's eye located? Where is the head part of a stalk barnacle?

12. Where are the barnacles' eggs before they get loose in the water?

13. What can you say of the size of barnacles? What color are barnacles?

14. Tell me what changes a barnacle makes during his life.

15. What part of a barnacle's life is like a crab's? What is a barnacle like in the larva stage?

16. When we mean more than one larva and pupa, what do we say? What sound do we give to the vowel digraph "ae" in these words? (long "e" sound)

17. What harm can barnacles do to ships?

Chapter Five
All About Jellyfish

Flowers of the Sea

Did you know that there are plants in the sea as well as on the land? Under the waves of the ocean, there are fields of green sea grasses, which look like lawns, and groves of great seaweeds, which look like trees. When scuba divers go down to the sea floor and walk about, they often find it hard to move in these tall plants; their feet get tangled in them. The divers feel as you would among the brush and vines of a great forest.

These splendid sea plants come in many colors and shapes. Some of the colors are red, pink, white, green, brown, purple, yellow, and orange. The leaves of these sea plants have many shapes. Some are round or long; others are flat or curly. Still others are cut into fine fingers; many are like fringes. They have spots, dots, or knobs upon them that shine like silver and gold.

The sea also has another kind of "flower." These are creatures that look more like lovely flowers than like anything else. We call them "sea flowers" and name some of them after dainty little plants that grow in the woods in spring. You must realize, however, that they are really sea creatures. It is these flower-like creatures that we shall study in this chapter.

You have read about insects and worms which are made in a ring pattern; now you will learn about these flower-like creatures which are made in a star pattern. This pattern is very simple, yet it is so built upon and changed that the members of this family are among the most lovely of animals. The ones that you learn about in this chapter are like a bicycle wheel with many spokes, which are called **rays**. These creatures have, from their odd and pretty shapes, such names as "sunflower," "aster," "fern," "crown," "fan," "pen," and so on.

Early one day, I went from my door to the beach, which was nearby, and there I saw a lovely object. The water was very still and clear, and floating in it was something all rose and cream color. This pretty thing was as large as a very large dinner plate. It was not flat but shaped like half an orange with the rounded side up. It was of a fine rose color and as clear as jelly. It looked much like pink jelly. From the center of the top to the edge went lines of a deeper pink. There were also dots around the outer edge. This edge seemed to have a soft, full ruffle of cream color about it. Looking closer, I saw that the underside was not flat. It was shaped like a bell, or an open **umbrella**. It had something which looked like long leaves, and which opened and shut.

Then I saw something else. From the darker lines on the upper part of the bell, long pink "arms" stretched out; these "arms" were almost a yard long. Their cream-colored edges had full ruffles, like soft lace. These long "arms" hung down in the water, and the water spread out their pretty edges. With a soft and gentle motion, they waved from side to side. In my boat I went quietly near this creature. It floated here and there, arrayed in all its beauty. I kept near it so I could watch it. This lovely thing was a **jellyfish**.

The jellyfish has a star pattern, but it has four—not five—rays. Its plan is like a large "X." If these rays are bent down, you will see that they form an upside down bowl. The ends of these four rays often run out

into arms, like the shape of a bell. All
the soft
pink and
c r e a m
jellylike
m a t t e r

X pattern

Bowl shape

Bell shape

fills the space between the upper part of the rays and
gathers into the ruffles along the edge. This is the
plan on which the jellyfish is built. Its frame is built
on four rays. The four parts between the rays may be
divided again so there are eight rays, instead of four.
Further, there may be sixteen rays instead of eight,
but the plan is always based on four.

The Life of a Jellyfish

The jellyfish belongs to the **hydroid** family of
creatures; this Latin name means "waterlike." The
jellyfish receives its common name from the clear
matter between the rays; this matter forms the bell
part of its body. It has also another name which
means "nettle"; it comes from the nettle plant. The
leaves of this plant can prick and sting your skin,
making it burn. The fine, long arms of the jellyfish
can sting in the same way.

The jellyfish is ninety-nine percent water, so its flesh
is as fluid as the white of an egg. If taken from the

water, jellyfish die in a very short time. They die by drying up; a very large jellyfish will dry to a thin, small skin. I do not know of any other living creature so soft or nearly all water, as a jellyfish. And yet these are real creatures of the sea. No doubt, they can hear, see, feel, and taste as other animals do.

All along the edge of the bell part you can see some dark dots, which are eyes. Some of the jellyfish have little eyes that are bare; that is, they have no lids or covers over them. These are called "bare-eyed jellyfish." Others have a little hood like a lid over each eye. Furthermore, along the bell part are little sacs which take the place of ears. The long arms which droop from the edge of the bell are the feelers with which they touch things. Their feelers wave gently to and fro and help the jellyfish to move through the water.

Up in the center of the underside of the bell is the mouth sac which has a little, fine frill over it. Even a jellyfish, you see, does not wish to keep its mouth wide open all the time. Below the mouth, the jellyfish has "fishing lines" or "nets," as the barnacle has. The soft, pretty ruffles move up and down in the water and catch things to put into its mouth. You would be surprised to know what large, hard things a soft jellyfish can soften and use as food. It can catch and eat fish, crabs, and shellfish. There is something in the jellyfish which helps dissolve these hard things. From its mouth sac, it often throws out the harder and larger shells and bones. It does this like you would remove nut shells or watermelon seeds from your mouth.

How do the jellyfish move in the water? They have no swimming feet, as crabs have, or fins, as fish have. Some of them move by spreading out the bell part of their bodies and then drawing it up again. This motion, which is like the rise and fall of your chest when you breathe, drives them through the water. Other jellyfish have a motion more like the opening and closing of the hands. Some have little oars, paddles, or hairs on the edge of the disk. Some seem to open and close as you would slowly open and shut an umbrella. The swimming bell of the jellyfish is often called the "umbrella" because of its shape.

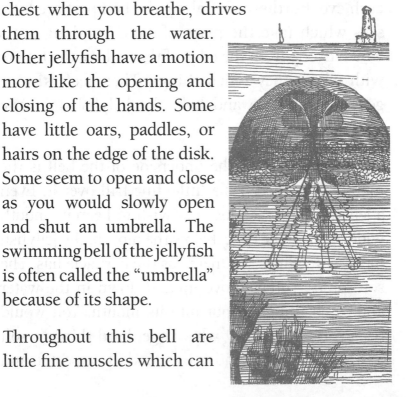

Throughout this bell are little fine muscles which can

spread out and draw together. There is also a flap called the **veil** on the underside of the swimming bell. This flap turns inward, and the little fine muscles spread over it. This veil is pulled together in the act of swimming and pushes out the water from the bell. Then the bell spreads and takes in more water, and again the water is driven out. A swimmer moves easily about the water by pushing it back with his arms; likewise, the jellyfish moves about as easily, even though it has no arms or legs.

I told you that jellyfish could sting. They can also shine. They can make a fine, bright light—something like glowworms or fireflies do, but more steady. From this power, they have been called "lamps of the sea." I have seen the ocean bright with them for miles. It looked as if all the stars had fallen from the sky, and were glowing in the water. When the jellyfish shine, the light is like a ball. It is not in long, straight lines or square. It is round like fireballs or balls of melted iron or glass. These balls are sometimes red, blue, white, green, or yellow.

Jellyfish differ much in size. Some are so small that you can hardly see them; others are as small as a split pea. Then some are the size of a dime, silver dollar, plate, and so on, up to the size of a huge wheel. As they are of many sizes, so they are of many shapes, as I told you. They are like balls, fans, bells, bottles, plumes, baskets, cups, or flowers.

And now, here is another odd thing to tell you. You know that when the barnacle is young it swims about. When it is grown up, it settles down to stay in

one place. The jellyfish is just the opposite. When it is young, it stays in one place and grows fast; but when it has grown up, it swims about wherever it chooses. I wonder which is the better way? Which way would you like best?

Some of the jellyfish come from an egg. Others come from what is called a "bud." Let us look at both of them. The egg at once fastens to some solid thing on the bottom of the sea. It grows into what looks like a plant with stems and branches. On these branches are little cup-shaped buds.

These buds are many little jellyfish growing on one stem. This is the larva stage. After a time, these buds open, and a young jellyfish breaks from the slender stem. At once, it goes swimming away, as happy as a jellyfish knows how to be.

Review

1. What are some of the names given to jellyfish? Why are they called jellyfish?

2. Why are they called "nettles"? Why are they given the names of flowers?

3. Can jellyfish live out of water? Describe what happens to them on land.

4. At what part of their lives are jellyfish fixed in one place?

5. What do jellyfish eat? How do they get their food? What do jellyfish use for fishing lines?

6. How do jellyfish move through the water?

7. Where are the eyes of jellyfish located? How do the eyes of jellyfish differ? Where are their mouths and ears?

8. Why have jellyfish been called "lamps of the sea"? What does the light of a jellyfish look like in the water?

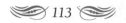

9. Describe the shape of jellyfish. What are some of the names which they get from their shapes? In what colors do jellyfish come?

10. On what plan is the body of a jellyfish made? How many rays are in the jellyfish pattern? Draw the rays of a jellyfish.

11. To what family do the jellyfish belong?

12. How much of a jellyfish's body is made of water?

13. If you have seen a jellyfish in the ocean, describe what it is like.

14. Should you touch a jellyfish if you see one in the ocean? Why?

Chapter Six
All About Sea Stars

Stars of the Sea

Now we come to another kind of sea creature which is made on the star plan. You may have seen pictures of them in the water, where they have their home. Are they not pretty things? The jellyfish gets one of its names from its shape and another name from its power to sting. Likewise, this "fish" gets one of its names from its shape—the **starfish**. It also gets a long, hard name from its coat.[1] Its coat is a thick, tough skin. On it are prickles much like those of a **hedgehog**. Most sea stars have five rays, or ten— because each single ray has been divided into two. All sea stars, however, do not keep to the plan of five. For example, the **sun star**—which is a splendid, bright-red color—has fourteen rays.

Grown-up sea stars show this shape most clearly, but it is never perfect; the young ones are only two-sided, not starlike. From their general shape, they

---

1. Its scientific name is *echinodermata* which means "hedgehog skin."

are called "stars"; from their skins, they are called "rough" or "hedgehog" coated. This skin is really their **exoskeleton**; they have their bones outside like the crabs and some other creatures. The crab's exoskeleton is hard, the sea star's is more like a tough skin filled with little spikes of shell-like matter. Sometimes

these little spikes lock together; at other times, they merely lie near each other, so some of the sea stars have much softer coats than the others. In the water, these coats are tough and bend like leather. When they are dry, they are brittle. If you want a dead sea star to bend, drop it into water.

Now I will tell you about three kinds of starfish. There is a strong, proper-looking starfish, with five points, called the **cross star**. There is another starfish with thin, crooked rays, or arms. It is called a **sand star** because it likes to lie close in the sand on the bottom of the sea. It is the color of sand. There is yet another with curled arms, like plumes, called the **brittle star**. This very strange fellow is called "brittle" because it breaks so easily. When things do not please it, the brittle star drops all to pieces. It would be a strange

Brittle
Star

thing if you could throw yourself down and break to pieces, snapping off your head, arms, and legs when you feel cross or afraid! Because of this unusual habit, it is very hard to get a brittle star out of the water. As soon as it feels a net, scoop, the sea air about it, or a pail of fresh water rising gently around it, it breaks into many pieces.

No doubt, you have heard how crabs can drop off a claw, and then another grows out. You also know that a spider does not mind much about losing a leg or two. These facts cause us to believe that these creatures do not suffer pain at the loss of a part of their bodies. If the loss of legs, claws, or rays caused pain, these creatures probably would not be so ready to loose them. There is no other creature that breaks itself so readily and so completely as the brittle star.

It will throw off all its rays, and they will float away in many directions while the little bell, or disk, is left alone to sink or to float. When this starfish loses one or more, or even four rays, others will soon grow. All the creatures of this family renew lost parts even more easily than crabs do.

Now we will look more closely at our model starfish, the **cross star**. It is our model because it is one of the most perfectly formed starfish God has made. Turn this creature over. Its mouth is in the center of the underside. If you look closely, there is a **seam**, or groove of the hard skin, all the way down the center of each ray. From the mouth, a nerve runs down to the point of each of the rays. On the end of every ray is a little sharp eye. Along the center of the seam on the bottom of each ray, there are numerous, little, blunt points. These points are like tiny tubes that are placed close together. It is on these that the starfish walks or creeps on the bottom of the sea or over rocks. The starfish seeks its food as it crawls slowly about. This sea star is very greedy; it is always hungry. It gives fishermen much trouble by eating fish bait right off their hooks. It also devours oysters. When it gets into an oyster bed, it is as bad as the drill. When an army of starfish go to a part of the coast where oysters grow, the oysters are soon killed.

Sea stars are of many bright, pretty colors. They may be green, brown, gray, red, pink, or with several colors on the same star. When they die, the flesh—which has much water in it—dries, and the tough, shell-like skin is left. You can dry them by pinning them on a board. Leave them for a few days in the sun and wind. If you do not pin out the rays, they may curl up.

A Sea Change

Starfish lay a great number of eggs. Let us see what happens to eggs of one kind of starfish. They are not dropped one by one into the water or strung on threads like chains. They stick to the underside of the parent starfish, which settles on the sand or rocks, resting on its back. It bends up its five rays, like a basket, to hold

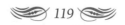

and protect the eggs. You see that in this position, the parent can neither walk nor eat. Although starfish are both greedy and restless, when they have eggs to take care of, they patiently lie quietly for ten days until the eggs hatch. In those ten days the parent starfish cannot eat or move. At the end of ten days, however, the larvae hatch and float away. Then the starfish finds that its work is done, and it turns back around and begins to walk, swim, and fish.

A most curious thing is the **lily star** egg, which fastens upon a coral or something firm and hard. Then it fastens itself as firmly as the barnacle on a rock. It shoots up a stem and, on the top of the stem, grows a cup like a lily blossom. It does not look like a starfish, but like a lovely lily. Fine plumes wave from its cup.

Sea Lilies

When the larvae first come from the eggs, many of them have no rays and do not look one bit like starfish. They look like tiny, barrel-like specks with little hairy hoops and a plume of hairs on one end. The hairs help the larvae swim through the water. Slowly they begin to change in shape and to lose their loops of hairs. All they want is to swim and to grow. When they are no larger than a flaxseed, or an eighth of an inch, they look like grown-up starfish. Some kinds of starfish have larvae that take other shapes. I cannot tell you about all of them, but I will tell of one kind. Only the **feather stars** attach themselves firmly to some object during the larva stage. In that stage, they do not look at all like the parent.

Finally, like the jellyfish, they change their shape, get loose, and swim off to explore their home—the wonderful world of the sea. Then they are like their parents.

Feather Star

Now let us take a closer look at our starfish. The little, tube-like things on the underside are all set in a groove. They are full of fluid, and each has a tiny sucker. The starfish can move them. These tube-like things serve not only for "feet" but also for "hands" to catch, hold, and kill their prey. Most of the starfish are dull and slow of motion. There is one kind, however, which moves quickly. It is called the **snake's-tail star** because of the shape of the rays, which are long and thin.

There is one kind of sea star often found on the coast of the Gulf of Mexico; it has all the space between the rays filled up with a hard, stony, or shell-like matter. It is like a flat box with five sides, so the shape of this creature is not like a star. There are some little loop holes completely through this hard box. On the middle of the top, there is the pattern of a five-pointed star. It is not a starfish, but a **sand dollar**. In this sea star, the disk spreads out, so as to include, or shut in, the rays. On the other hand,

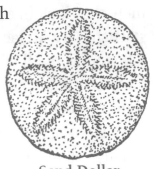

Sand Dollar

there are some sea stars that have the disk very small. They seem to be all rays and no disk. People who have studied sea stars divide them into six families. I have told you about most of them. There is one family that is of such a strange shape that they are called "cucumbers"—**sea cucumbers**. The Chinese like to eat them, and ships are sent out to fish for them. They grow in the shallows near the islands in tropic seas.

Sea Cucumber

The Sea Star with an Overcoat

There is a very pretty starfish called the "sea egg," or **sea urchin**. This creature does not have five points, or rays; it is in the shape of a ball, somewhat flattened. You might ask, "Can this belong to the sea star family, when it has no rays?" Well, let us see. Look at the first picture which represents our basic ray pattern. Bend the rays up, and the plan looks like the second

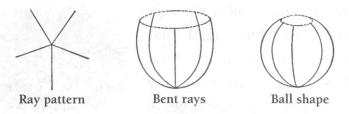

Ray pattern	Bent rays	Ball shape

picture. Then bend them until the tips nearly touch, and you have the form of the third picture. The cover of the sea urchin is not tough and skinlike; it is hard and shell-like. If you look closely, you will see that it has, up and down its coat, lines of knobs and dots set in double rows. You will find five double lines of large knobs, and as many lines of small dots between the larger ones. Do not think that you can see these marks as soon as you find a sea urchin? By no means! The sea urchin wears a fine, thick overcoat, which hides its shell.

I knew a boy who found a number of sea urchins lying on the beach. He cried out, "Oh! look at all the chestnut burs in the water!" When it is alive, the sea urchin looks a lot like a chestnut bur—ripe, but not open. This sea star is covered

Chestnut bur

all over with thorns, or prickles, just like the bur, and it gets its dark brown color from the water.

Now let us look into this
matter. You have read that
a cross star has many little
tubes full of something like
water along the under edges of
its rays. It can move them and

Common Sea Urchin

use them to walk. On the other hand, the sea urchin
has hard, sharp spines, which cover all the shell, and
look like a rough coat. In the pictures, you see the
sea urchin with its shell bare, with its shell half bare,
and with its full overcoat of spines, or **quills**. When
the shell is bare, you will see little lines of points or
knobs all over it. These are very pretty, but they are for
a special use, not just for their beauty. On every tiny
knob is placed a spine, and the sea urchin can turn
and move its spines in all directions, just as easily as
you can move your arm at the shoulder joint. When

the urchin is alive, the spines, or quills, stand out all about it. After it dies, the quills drop off. There are five double rows of holes, like pinpricks, between the rows of knobs. Out of these holes grow tiny suckers, as I told you the starfish had.

The sea urchin walks on its spines, as the cross star does on its spines. Since the quills of the urchin are all around it, like a ball cover, its walk is a roll! By the little suckers, it can cling to the rocks and climb up their sides. Turn over the bare urchin shell, and you will see that, while at the top it has no opening larger than a pinprick, there is a hole on the underside where the curved rays do not come entirely together. You see the urchin must have this opening for its fish lines and to put food into its ever-hungry mouth.

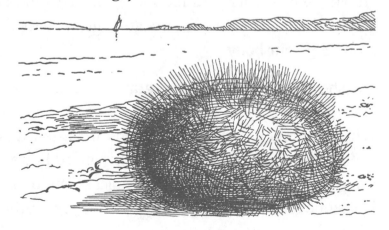

Since the sea urchin eats so much, it must grow! Does it? Yes, the sea urchin grows, and it cannot cast its shell as a crab can. It does not have a soft skin as you have, yet his shell is never too tight. How can the shell expand as the sea urchin grows? The shell is made up of a great many little plates, or scales. As the urchin within grows and needs more room, these little scalelike plates grow larger all around. It is interesting that these tiny plates are set like bricks in a dome. You know the sea urchin is made on the five-ray pattern, bent like a flattened ball. Around the body of the sea urchin—within its shell—is wrapped a soft, pretty, silklike **mantle**. This mantle lines the shell. It takes lime from the seawater and builds it into more shell along the five edges of these tiny plates. It also adds new plates. So, as the urchin keeps growing all the time, its mantle is building upon the plates all the time. The coat grows with the growth of its owner. I think your mother would be glad if she could find you a coat to grow with the growth of your body.

The shell part of the urchin is gray or greenish gray. The quills are often red, brown, pink, or purple. When a number of these sea urchins are fastened on a rock, they look like a bed of lovely fringed flowers. Some sea urchins are able to bore holes, even in hard limestone rock in which they live. As they grow, they make the holes larger, but not the openings. After a time, they are shut into a prison which they have dug for themselves. They do not do this, however, along the coast of North America. On

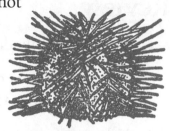

Boring Sea Urchin

the coast of Spain, you will find the rocks covered with these urchins, fixed in holes. No doubt, they feel that stone walls are safe. If they had wished to get away, and go and come freely, I think they could have made their doorways as large as themselves.

In some places, the sea urchins are small—not much larger than a dime. In warmer seas, the urchins grow large, even as large as a large orange. People there often use these larger ones for food.

There is much more to be learned about sea urchins. You will do well to study them when you can. In fact, the oldest person alive has not lived long enough to learn all there is to know about these very simple and common creatures. There is danger that, when we have learned a little bit about God's creation, we become proud and do not take the trouble to learn more of His wonderful works.

Review

1. To what family do sea stars belong?

2. How many rays do most sea stars have? How many rays does the sun star have?

3. What can you tell me about brittle stars? How do the brittle stars protect themselves?

4. What kind of coat or skin does a starfish have? Where is its mouth?

5. Do starfish swim or crawl? What colors do starfish have? What do they eat?

6. Why is the cross star a model starfish? How does the cross star hatch its eggs?

7. What does the starfish look like when it leaves the egg? Which starfish grows fast in the larva stage?

9. Describe the spines on the underside of a starfish.

10. How many kinds of sea stars can you describe? What is a sea cucumber?

11. What is a sea urchin? Draw the sea urchin pattern. To what family does it belong?

12. Describe the sea urchin's overcoat, quills, and suckers.

13. Describe the size and color of sea urchins. How does the urchin's shell increase in size?

14. How does the sea urchin walk and climb? When are sea urchins and sea cucumbers eaten?

15. Describe the shell of a sea urchin when the quills are gone. Where is the sea urchin's mouth?

16. Describe how some sea urchins bore holes in rock. What do they do as they grow?

All Things Beautiful

All things bright and beautiful,
All creatures great and small,
All things wise and wonderful,—
The Lord God made them all.

Each little flower that opens,
Each little bird that sings,
He made their glowing colors,
He made their tiny wings.

The purple-beaded mountain,
The river, running by,
The morning, and the sunset
That lighteth up the sky.

The tall trees in the green wood,
The pleasant summer sun,
The ripe fruits in the garden,
He made them every one.

He gave us eyes to see them,
And lips that we might tell

How great is God Almighty,
Who hath made all things well.

John Keble

Chapter Seven
All About Dragonflies

The Flying Flowers

You have just read about some members of the sea star family. From their beauty they have been called "flowers of the sea." We will now learn about some insects which might be called "flying flowers." I knew a boy who, the first time that he noticed butterflies, cried out, "Oh, see all those flowers flying!" That was a cute reply because it describes the butterflies well.

There is another family of insects which also deserves the name of "flying flowers." Their shape, colors, and motions are very lovely. These insects are the **dragonflies**. They are also called horse-stingers, darning-needles, spindles, and so on. These beautiful creatures have been given some harsh names, but they never harm anyone or anything—except for small flying insects. Perhaps the way they treat these smaller insects is why they have been given such names.

The French people call these insects "little ladies." Now that is a nicer name. It is given to them because they are graceful and pretty, and also neat and delicate, in their looks and motions. I knew a man who called them "air jewels" because they are almost always in flight, and their eyes and bodies flash and shine like precious gems.

Nevertheless, I have known silly people to jump and scream when one of these dragonflies came darting by. That was foolish, because they might as well scream at a rose or a violet. There is no need of running away from them. The only time you will have trouble with dragonflies is when you want to examine them. Since they are so swift and shy, you will not be able to catch one!

Dragonflies are similar to the termites, **mayflies**, and **lacewings**. They have four large, fine, lacelike wings—each divided into a great many spaces, or meshes. Both pairs of wings are nearly equal in size. Their heads are large, and their light bodies are long. Dragonflies are also very active in their moves and are very seldom at rest. They fly so swiftly that you can scarcely see their thin wings; only the flash of their bright-colored bodies is visible.

Dragonflies like damp or wet places. You will find them above lakes and ponds. They fly over marshy places or by the edges of quiet streams. Go out to some still, silvery pond where the tall trees stand in a ring about the water. The ferns, the tall yellow spikes of the St.-John's-wort, and the blue clubs of the arrow plant make a wreath around the sandy shore. There you will see hundreds of lively dragonflies darting up and down. They swing in the sunbeams, as if glad to be alive. In their great beauty, they are as pretty as the butterflies. Like the butterflies, dragonflies love the sunshine and are the children of the summer. The hotter the weather, the happier they seem to be.

Let us look more closely at a dragonfly. It belongs to the class of the ring-made creatures. Its long, slim body is made in rings, and its feet and legs are jointed. Some kinds of dragonflies have a rather flat body, but usually it is round, and it is thinnest in the middle, and thickens a little at the tail and where it joins the chest, or thorax.

The wings of the dragonfly are tough and of iris or golden hues. Sometimes the body is a vivid blue or bright green. Sometimes it is banded or spotted with yellow or scarlet. Its wide wings look like delicate lace spread on a fine frame. A little child, who found one of these wings, brought it to me saying, "I got a good piece of lace!"

The head of the dragonfly is large and has what is called a **compound eye** on each side. Like that of the housefly, this compound eye is made up of many eyes set so closely together that they seem to be one; there are over twelve thousand tiny eyes in only one compound eye.

Compound Eye

Through these amazing eyes, the light plays and flashes like fire. Between the compound eyes, three little **simple eyes** are set in a line across the head. The dragonfly's head also has a strange mouth. Its jaws are hidden under two thin, skinlike lips. These move up and down as it eats. It does not suck food, like the butterflies and houseflies, but eats after the manner of the beetle. You see, the dragonfly belongs to the great division of the "eaters," not of the "drinkers." Instead of feeding on nectar, as we would think such lovely things should, they eat insects.

All its life long, from the moment it hatches, it is always greedy because it is always hungry. It spends all its time hunting for food. Who could count how many small insects a dragonfly eats in its short lifetime?

Living Under the Water

Now let us hear the story of the dragonfly from its beginning. While it is an egg and later a larva, or **nymph**, it lives under the water. Only after molting several times does it burst forth with its wings and leave the water, seeking the air above. As a larva, the dragonfly lives in cool, still shallows among green and graceful water plants. There the sunshine glows all about it, as it darts over the bottom of the pond, hunting for food.

The mother dragonfly, as she flits over the water, drops

her eggs on it, and they sink to the bottom. At times, she may put them into plant stems. Their cases are waterproof. If the eggs are not eaten up by beetles and other underwater creatures, they are quite safe, and soon the larvae hatch out. They look much like adult dragonflies but without wings. Many insects go through four stages of metamorphosis (egg, larva, pupa, and adult), but dragonflies only go through three stages (egg, larva, and adult). They remain in the larva stage until they become adults. At first the larvae, or **nymphs**, move about rather slowly and lazily. As they grow, they become stronger and more active. Then they begin to dash here and there, frightening all the little creatures in the pond. At last, the adult insects rise on their wings, darting about at what seems like the speed of light.

The larva of the dragonfly is gray and has six legs. It is always hungry and feeds on small water creatures, such as beetles, grubs, shrimp, leeches, and their young. This nymph does not run after its food, but lies waiting for it. On the bottom of the pond—hidden in the shadow of a leaf, root, or stone; or seated on stems or leaves that are under water—the larva waits patiently for its prey to come by. When it seizes food, the larva likes to strike it from below, rising under its prey, as the shark does. The dragonfly larva is very bold; it can eat insects that are large and hard.

Did you ever see a person with a net for catching insects? This net is a fine bag attached to a little hoop. The hoop is fastened upon a long handle. Sometimes the handle has joints that will fold up. As insects dart by, the person with the net brings it down over them with one quick move. The dragonfly larva catches its food with a "net" in much the same way. Its lower jaw is fastened by a hinge to a little jointed rod. When not in use, the rod and the jaw plate, which is on the end of the rod, are folded on the head of the insect. This plate has fine teeth on its edge.

When prey comes by, the larva snaps out its rod with the plate, as if they both were on a spring. In this way, the larva catches its food as it swims along.

Dragonfly Larva

The prey does not see its foe and does not know that the larva can reach so far with its "sweep net." The teeth on the edge of the plate close, and then the rod snaps back and puts the food into the hungry larva's throat. I suppose the little creatures that swim along feel quite happy and safe; but then, all at once, out springs this weapon, and they are gone.

This little plague of the pond, however, is not quite safe himself. There are some other creatures down under the water that eat him. God designed all of creation to work in this way, one group of living things or creatures feeding on another group. Dragonflies are part of this food chain. The **food chain** begins with green plants, which provide food for other plants, animals, and people; each depends on the next plant or animal for food. In this way, God provides for all living plants, animals, and people.

The dragonfly nymph breathes air. It has no lungs as you have, but **gills** as a fish has. How does it get air? A long tube goes through its body and ends in a hornlike point at the tail. This point is made of five very fine spikes. These spikes and this tube are able to take tiny bubbles of air from the water. In this way, it gets air more or less as a fish does.

The spike on the larva's tail has a very important use. It shoots out the water which it has taken in, as you would shoot water from a squirt gun. It shoots the water out with such power that it drives the larva along in the water. Did you ever see a steamboat driven through the water by a wheel at the **stern**, or back part, of the boat? The man who first invented the steamboat said that he took his idea of how it should be made by seeing the larva of the dragonfly move in the water.

As the dragonfly larva grows and molts (sheds its exoskeleton), it becomes more lively, fierce, and hungry than ever. At this time, it does not change its form as much as most insects do. The nymph has six legs, and each foot has strong hooks on it. Its clear, shining color is pale brown, and its exoskeleton is strong and hard. Some rings of the body have hornlike spikes upon them. On the thorax, there is a pattern like wings.

The nymph dashes about the bottom of the pond, swimming or running, and eats almost everything that lives there. The body and head of the nymph are thicker than those of the grown-up dragonfly. They are made for seizing and killing prey. When it is nearly time for the nymph to come out as an adult dragonfly, it gets ready to molt for the last time. Its large, beautiful eyes grow brighter and brighter, and the nymph leaves the deeper part and gets near the edge of the pond.

A Happy Change

When the end of the larva stage draws near, the coming dragonfly loses its fierce appetite. It seems to feel tired and heavy. It breathes slowly, as if it cannot get air enough. The body has changed inside the hard case, and the time is near when it will leave the water for the air, and swimming for flying. Once the nymph wanted nothing better than to chase and eat creatures underwater. Now, all at once, it longs to fly freely in the air and enjoy the warmth of the sun.

The dragonfly nymph needs no one to tell it what to do. By God's design, it knows exactly how it should act. This tired larva now seeks the stem of some tall reed or grass that grows in the water. Slowly it crawls up the stem. The hooks on its feet firmly hold the larva as it goes, and it keeps on going until it is nearly a **meter** above water. The hooks, though very small, are so sharp and hard that they can go into wood. When the nymph is as high up as it wants to be, it drives the hooks into the stem. Thus it will hold firm even when it twists and struggles hard.

The nymph likes best to find two reeds or stems near to each other, so that it can take hold of both and swing between the two. Then, like a child in a swing, it begins to sway back and forth. Now, as it sways, a strange thing happens. Its hard larval case splits open down its back. Look! Inside the old exoskeleton, we see a perfect insect with its wings! The old case is firmly held by the hooked feet, while the changed insect twists and pulls until it is nearly free. Little by little, its head, legs, wings, and long body come forth; and finally, the case hangs only by the last ring of the insect's body. If you look for these old cases, you will often find them clinging to the reeds by a pond.

Perhaps you would think the dragonfly was dead. For after it stretches out—first one leg and then the other—it hangs by its last ring, stiff and still. It is not dead; it is only resting. After about fifteen minutes it awakes. Taking a firm hold with its feet upon a stem or leaf, it lets go of its hold upon the old exoskeleton. The old case is left hanging by its hooks in its place. Now here is a dragonfly, with its large head, two compound eyes, six legs, four wings, and long, dull body! And now, at last, it can breathe freely through all those tubes and air-holes which are on an adult insect's body.

Still the insect does not look like a full-grown dragonfly. Its colors are dull, and its wings are folded up. The body is soft, damp, and too short. Its big eyes are dim. As if half asleep, it still clings to the stem, not far from the case which is the old shape of itself. The new insect is drawing in the sunshine and fresh air. It stands still and breathes hard, filling its new body with pure, dry air. Now and then its wings quiver. As they quiver, they spread out, fold after fold, as silken banners wave out in the air. Then at last they are spread out wide, in all their beauty.

The dragonfly has reached its last and highest stage. It can sail away where it pleases on its new wings. As the wings grow larger, the eyes of the dragonfly grow brave and bright; its body dries. Then it gleams like a jewel. Its fresh colors come out clearly. It feels strong and active. Then, all at once, it uses its new wings. It rises into the air and flashes here and there, just as hungry and ten times swifter than ever before. The dragonfly eats almost every kind of creature which you have read about so far, and more! It likes to eat beetles, spiders, flies, centipedes, freshwater shrimp, and **tadpoles**—or "polliwogs," as some people call them.

The dragonfly larvae live for about a year, but grown-up dragonflies live only a part of one summer. You will find most dragonflies in July or August; however, when the frost comes, they die. After dragonflies have died, the great beauty of their bodies passes away quickly. They fade and grow dull, as when they first came from their larval cases. The scarlet, yellow, blue, or green turns to a drab color. Because of this, you cannot keep them as well as you can keep beetles. It is life that gives the dragonfly its splendid beauty.

The Dragonfly, Damselfly, and Lacewing

The flight of the dragonfly is called **hawking**, for it moves like that powerful bird called the hawk. The dragonfly is fond of chasing other insects, but since it flies so swiftly, it does not need a long jaw set on a rod, as the larva had. In flight, the dragonfly seems to catch and tear its prey for the mere pleasure of pulling them to pieces. If it gets caught in a place where its wide wings cannot turn or might be injured, it simply flies backwards and gets off safely. It also fights with other dragonflies and has some hard battles.

Few insects are so fast in flight as this, and few have such beauty. Their eyes are beautiful for the clear, glowing light in them; the body, for its vivid color; and their wings, for their lacelike texture. Each of the wings has a dark spot on the front edge. Often, in flying, this spot and the line of bright color of the dragonfly's body—almost like a streak of fire—are all that can be seen of the insect. Yet, after all has been said, I think that the main beauty of the dragonfly is in its eyes. They are like two great, flaming jewels.

There are several kinds of dragonflies. These are different in color and size, and in the shapes of their bodies. One, with a very long, thin, dark body, is called the "darning needle." One, with a thicker body, is called the "ringed club." Its body is largest at the tail end. This one is dressed in black and gold, and it is large and strong.

A smaller insect similar to the dragonfly, which has no spots on the wings,   is called the damselfly. This kind is among the prettiest of all. Some of them are bright red, and others are a clear, light blue. They look more like creatures in some fairy

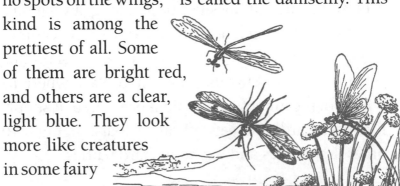

tale than like real live insects because they flit here and there like streaks of bright-colored light. You can scarcely see the wings on which they fly.

There is an even smaller insect similar to the dragonfly called the **lacewing**. The head and body of the lacewing are bright green,

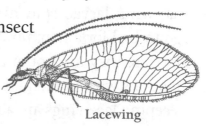

Lacewing

its wings are like white **gauze**; but its main beauty is in its eyes. Some call it "golden eyes" because its eyes are like a drop of amber, or melted gold. The veins in the wings of the lacewing are very fine. As the light falls on the wings, they change in color and look like pink, red, blue, green, or gold threads.

This lovely lacewing does not like the bright light of the midday sun, as the dragonfly does. It prefers to come out in the moonlight, or when the sun is setting. Moreover, the lacewing is not a water lover, as the dragonfly is. It lays its eggs on leaves, and every egg is held upon a little silken stem. The stem is much like the silk which the spider spins. These eggs are laid in groups.

When the young larvae come out of their eggs, they feed on the little aphids.

Lacewing

Eggs

Pupa Case

Do you remember that the aphids make the honeydew that honey ants like so much? In two weeks these lacewing larvae change to pupae. To do this the lacewing larvae spin nice silk balls in which they go to bed for a nap; now they are in the pupa stage. In this, they are not at all like the young dragonfly nymphs which hunt and swim about. The balls of the sleeping lacewings are about the size of a mustard or poppy seed.

The lacewings are short-lived. Only one summer makes a lifetime for them. In a summer, they grow from infancy to old age, making all their changes and living out their time as adult insects. After the lacewing dies, it loses all its fine colors in a very few hours.

The Wings of the Dragonfly

We can find no better example than the dragonfly, of the way in which insects behave when they leave the larval case. You know that this case is tough and always seems smaller than the grown-up insect; so, the insect must be very closely packed in. No person could pack an adult insect back into the case it has just left.

While the dragonfly larva is underwater, the case is kept tough, and yet soft enough to bend. When the nymph, however, crawls up the stem of the plant into the air, the case soon dries and becomes brittle. As the dragonfly struggles within, the dry case will easily split. The little wet coat, which covers the body while it is in the case, makes it easier to slip out of the shell when it cracks open. Likewise, if you have on your finger a ring which is too tight, you can pull it off if you wet your finger. The wet coat that covers the dragonfly in the case keeps the wings from being hurt by their tight folding. After they are dry and spread out, they are easy to break. Then it is very easy to hurt or spoil them.

The dragonfly seems to know this, and is careful of its wings. In the act of unfolding, the dragonfly holds its wings from touching any object, even its own body. When the dragonfly gets free from the case, it knows just how to spread its lovely wings into perfect shape. It stands quite still and far enough from stems

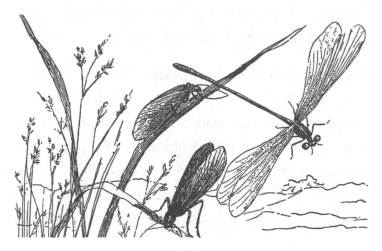

or leaves to keep its wide wings safe. The dragonfly does not move its wings but lets the air do the work, while it holds its bent body away from the wings. The quiver you see through it, now and then, is a motion of the body.

When the dragonfly first comes from the case, its wings are soft, and will bend as easily as wet paper. After they are dry, they are like thin plates of glass. These wings have very many nerves through them. Their frame is like a fine network, and, as it is touched by the air, it spreads slowly to its full size. During this drying time, if the wings are hurt, they will never come to their right shape. If anyone should try to help a dragonfly out of its case, its wings would be ruined and never take their right shape. Human hands are too clumsy for such work.

When the dragonfly first comes from the case, the wings and body are of a dull, faded color; but as it stands in the sun and air, you can see it change from minute to minute. Fold after fold of the wings shakes out; ring after ring of the body stretches to its proper length; the joints of the legs come to their right shape and firmness. From all the body of the insect a mist seems to pass away; and the colors of the dragonfly come out—red, blue, green, and gold shine in beauty.

Now let us look closely at these fine, wide wings. Although they are so thin, like gauze, yet they are double. There is a surface on each side, spread over a very fine frame. The parts of this frame are small as the finest hairs; even though they are so tiny, they are all hollow. They are tubes or pipes that carry air and a very thin, white fluid—which is the blood of the insect—through the wings. Now that you know this, can you clearly see how the wings expand? As soon as the dragonfly comes out of its larval case, air and thin fluid are driven through these fine tubes. As they fill, they stretch out, and the thin surface which covers them spreads with them.

If you notice the dragonfly as its wings take shape, you will see that quiver which I spoke of. That motion is the pumping of air and fluid through its tubes, by which the fly spreads out its wings and its body. The dragonfly spends about fifteen minutes in getting into shape. Sometimes half an hour is needed. After that, the fly rests for an hour or two before it tries its wings in the air. Very likely, it wishes to give its wings time to get quite firm and hard. Butterflies, lacewings, mayflies, and other insects of the kind have their wings made in this way; so what you learn about one will help you to understand the others.

Mayflies

The **mayflies** are very pretty insects. Once I was on a large island, on a day when mayflies had come out; the air was full of their shining, silvery shapes—they landed on people's clothes and seemed to cover them with a gauze veil. They are similar to dragonflies but very much smaller, and mayflies are not fond of tearing up other insects. You will find them in moist places. Their bodies are much slimmer than those of dragonflies. Their wings are unequal, and their heads are smaller. Mayflies have two front legs, nearly as long as the body, which are held almost straight out as they fly. On their tails, they have three long, stiff hairs, twice as long as the body. These hairs spread out in the shape of a fan.

These insects are often called mayflies because they usually come in the month of May; but they have another name which means the "child of an hour." This name is given them because they seldom live longer than one day—and often only for an hour or two. In the egg and larva stages, they live about two years; but, once they receive their wings, they soon die.

How do they spend that short life? They do not eat, for they have no mouths. As they are not hungry, they do not hunt. They spend their whole time in flying. Their flight is a sort of dance in the air; they rise and fall, and spin about. Great numbers of them come out together, spin about,

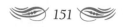

151

and drop their eggs in the water; but soon they flutter down, dead, among the grasses. That is the story of the pretty mayfly. Would you not like to seek out in their homes, and then read and study about, the very many strange and wonderful insects that are in the world?

Mayfly

Review

1. What insects have been called "flying flowers"? What are some of the names given to dragonflies?

2. Can a dragonfly do you any harm?

3. Name some insects that have lacelike wings similar to the dragonfly.

4. Describe a dragonfly, especially their wonderful eyes.

5. What kind of places and weather do dragonflies like? What do they eat?

6. What is the flight of dragonflies called?

7. Is the dragonfly an "eater" or a "drinker"?

8. Where does the dragonfly live while an egg and larva? How do a dragonfly's eggs get into the water?

9. Describe the larva's strange mouth and how it catches its food.

10. How does the larva get air while it lives under water?

11. Where did the pattern of a stern wheel on a steamboat come from?

12. Describe the metamorphosis of a dragonfly. How does the larval case change before the dragonfly comes out?

13. Describe how the nymph leaves the water so it can change into an adult dragonfly.

14. What are the hooks on its feet used for? In what way does the adult get free of its case?

15. Describe the wings of the dragonfly. How does it take care of its wings?

16. How long does the dragonfly live in the larva stage? In the adult stage?

17. What can you say of the way the dragonfly hunts insects?

18. Describe a lacewing. Where does the lacewing lay its eggs?

19. What do lacewing larvae eat? How long do adult lacewings live?

20. Do dragonflies and lacewings keep their colors when dead?

21. Describe how the adult dragonfly expands its wings. Why will the wings bend when they first come from the old case?

22. Describe mayflies. How long do they live in the adult stage? Do they eat? How do they spend their short lives?